目次

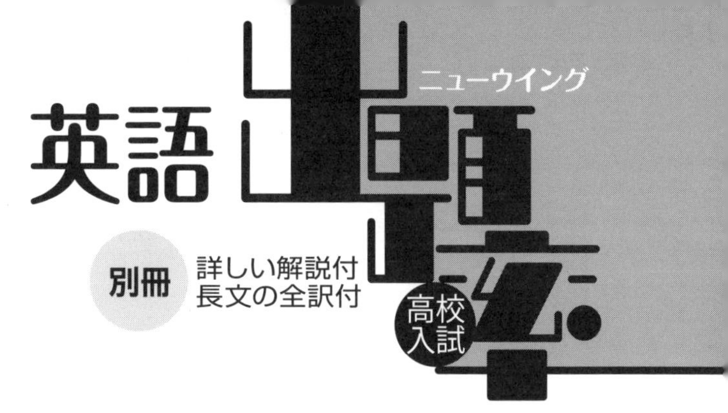

（注） 本書の内容についての一切の責任は英俊社にございます。ご不審の点は当社へご質問下さい。（編集部）

出題率って、どういう意味

その単元が入学試験に出題される割合で、
入試対策を効率よく進めるために役立つ情報です。

$$\text{出題率}(\%)=\frac{\text{その単元が出題された試験数}}{\text{調査した全試験数}}\times 100$$

英俊社の「高校別入試対策シリーズ」出版校のすべての問題を、過去3年さかのぼって調査、算出しています。

この本のねらい

この本を手にする受験生の皆さんの中には，高校入試に向けて，いったい何をどのように勉強すればよいのか悩んでいる人も多いことでしょう。もちろん，すべての単元の内容を徹底的に勉強しておけば，実際の入試で十分合格点を取れることは誰もが知っています。しかし，過去の入試問題を見ればわかるように，「**入試で出題されやすい**」内容というものがあります。これを念頭に置いて学習するのとそうでないのとでは，同じ努力でも得られる効果がかなり違ってくると思われます。

この本は，『高校別入試対策シリーズ〈赤本〉』（英俊社）出版校の入試問題を独自の項目で分類して**出題率**を算出し，「**入試で出題されやすい**」内容にねらいを定めた構成としています。入試の実態に即した学習をめざす皆さんには，きっと大きな力になるでしょう。

この本の特長

◆例題で単元チェック　⇒　STEP UP　で問題演習

各単元のはじめに例題がのせてあります。典型的な問題を取り上げていますので，まずは実力のチェックをしてください。例題の解説には重要なポイントのまとめも掲載しています。その後，実践的な問題演習を行いましょう。

◆出題率の高い問題に的をしぼっているので，効果的な問題演習が行える

高校入試で出題率の高い問題（＝よく出会う問題）に的をしぼって収録しています。また，出題率の高い順に掲載していますので，より効率のよい入試対策ができます。

◆長文問題も効率的に学習ーよく出るテーマの問題演習ー

「1．長文問題」の問題演習では，入試でよく出るテーマの長文を取り上げています。「物語」「人物」「文化」などのテーマに慣れておくことで，長文をよりスムーズに読むことができます。

◆ポイントをおさえた解説

解くことができなかった問題や間違えた問題はじっくりと解説を読みましょう。また，長文問題の解説には全訳もついていますので，ぜひ活用してください。

入試に向けての対策

この本は上記の方針に基づいてつくられているので，まずは何度もくり返し取り組み，出題の傾向をつかんで下さい。そのうえで，まだ理解が足りないと感じたところや，この本に収録されていない単元についても学習を重ねて下さい。その際に，英俊社の『**英語の近道問題シリーズ**』をぜひ活用して下さい。また，出題率の集計結果はあくまでも全般的傾向になりますので，「出会いやすい」単元の内容を把握するだけでなく，志望校において「好んで出題される」単元や出題形式を知っておくことも大切になってきます。そこで〈赤本〉でおなじみのベストセラー『**高校別入試対策シリーズ**』（英俊社）を入念に仕上げて，万全の態勢で入試に向かって下さい。

単元分類と出題率集計

調査対象校：253校　総試験数：874試験

大単元	出題試験数	出題率(%)	順位	小単元	出題試験数	出題率(%)	順位
音　声	207	23.7	7	語の発音	155	17.7	9
				語のアクセント	127	14.5	10
				文の区切り·強勢	21	2.4	16
語　い	243	27.8	6	相関関係表(語の変化)	84	9.6	12
				単　語	190	21.7	7
英文法	585	66.9	3	語形変化	65	7.4	13
				英文完成選択	451	51.6	2
				英文完成補充	38	4.3	15
				同意文完成	221	25.3	5
				指示による文の書き換え	47	5.4	14
				正誤判断	98	11.2	11
英作文	732	83.8	2	整序作文	522	59.7	1
				和文英訳	230	26.3	4
				その他の英作文	325	37.2	3
読　解	334	38.2	5	問答·応答	215	24.6	6
				英文和訳	1	0.1	17
				絵や表を見て答える問題	178	20.4	8
会話文	552	63.2	4				
長文問題	843	98.8	1				
放送問題	480	54.9					

※大単元の集計は，一試験中に重複して出題されている小単元を除外しています。

出題項目の出題率集計

上の表は，主に「**出題形式**」に着目して分類しています。英語では，それ以外に文法的な「**出題項目**」によって，学習を進める場合もあります。そこで，文法的な項目の出題率を調査してみると，右の表のようになります。

出題率の高い文法項目については，特に重点的に学習しておく必要があるでしょう。

項　目		出題率	順位
基本時制	343	53.2	7
比　較	465	72.1	2
現在完了	404	62.6	3
受動態	403	62.5	4
不定詞	515	79.8	1
動名詞	325	50.4	8
分　詞	296	45.9	10
関係代名詞	320	49.6	9
命令文	162	25.1	11
感嘆文	33	5.1	14
特殊な疑問文	367	56.9	6
特殊な否定文	115	17.8	12
文型	382	59.2	5
仮定法	34	5.3	13

※1　付加疑問文・間接疑問・否定疑問文など
※2　二重否定・準否定・部分否定など
※3　There is/are ～・2文型・4文型・5文型など

この本の使い方

例 題

長文問題・英作文・英文法・会話文のそれぞれのテーマについて，どういった問題が出題されることが多いのかを，実際の入試問題で示しています。
まずは自分の力でチャレンジしてみましょう。

例題の解説には，問題の解き方を詳しくのせてあります。どうやって答えにたどりつくのかをしっかりと確認しておきましょう。

＋plus α や **アドバイス** には得点アップにつながる知識や考え方をまとめています。ぜひ参考にしてください。

【答】 各例題には答えがのせてあります。間違った問題は，特に解説をしっかりと読み，理解を深めましょう。

STEP UP 例題を解き，解説を読み終わったら，問題演習を行いましょう。ここには，英俊社の「赤本」から選び抜かれた良問が，たくさん収録されています。何度も解いて，実力をつけましょう。

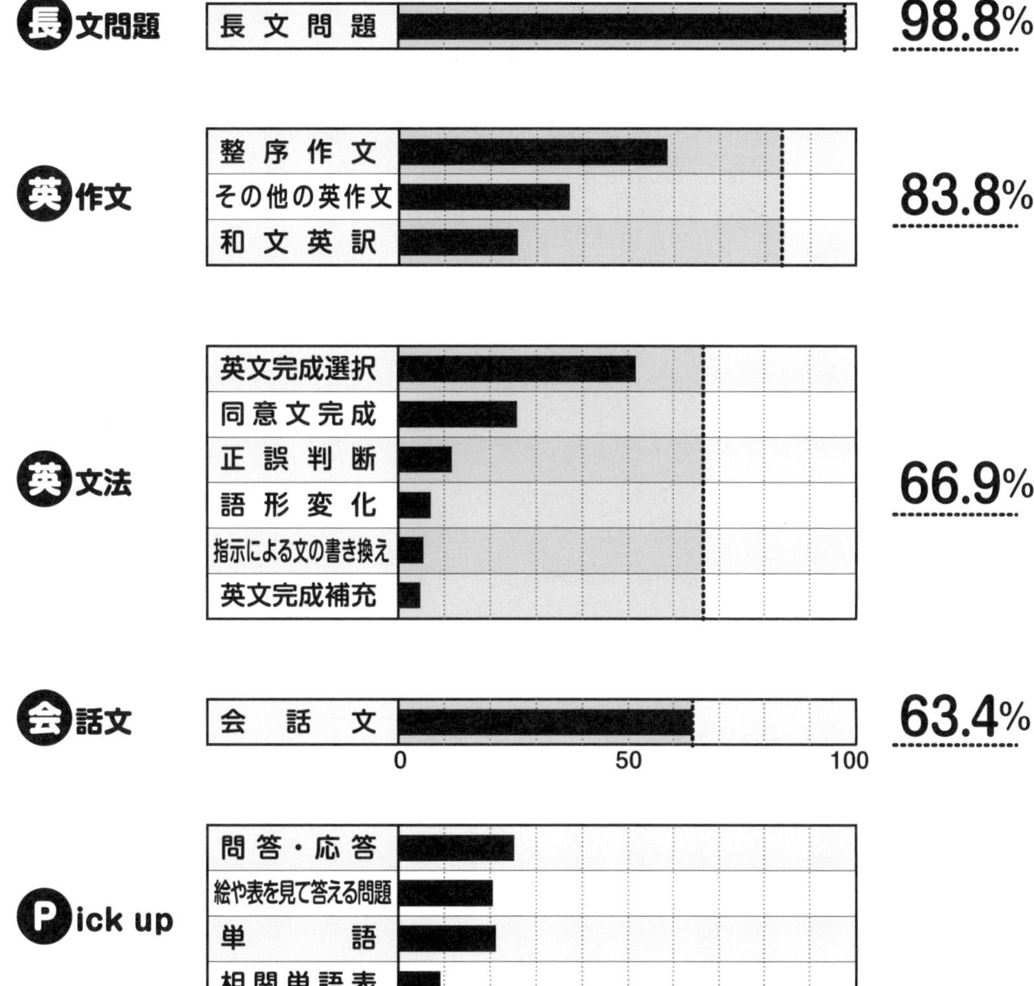
0
50
100
長文問題
長文問題
98.8%
英作文
整序作文
その他の英作文
和文英訳
83.8%
英文法
英文完成選択
同意文完成
正誤判断
語形変化
指示による文の書き換え
英文完成補充
66.9%
会話文
会話文
63.4%
0
50
100
Pick up
問答・応答
絵や表を見て答える問題
単語
相関単語表

1 長文問題

ニューウイング出題率 98.8%

例題1　よく出る問題形式の解き方を身につけよう

□ 次の英文を読んで，あとの問いに答えなさい。（大阪商大高）

Yayoi is thirteen years old. She is a junior high school student. Her school is an hour from her house by train. Her mother makes sandwiches for her breakfast every morning, but she is not good at ① (get) up early and she has no time to eat breakfast in the morning. So she brings ② <u>them</u> to school.

Yayoi eats the sandwiches during lunch time. *In short, she doesn't eat breakfast every day.

One day, Yayoi suddenly felt sick in class. She quickly went to the nurse's room, and she didn't know the reason. The teacher asked her, "Did you eat breakfast today?" "No, I don't eat breakfast every day. Why do you ask?" Yayoi answered.

"Eating breakfast *affects your *school performance. You need a lot of energy for school activities, don't you? Thanks for eating breakfast, we can get the power for everyday life," the teacher said.

Yayoi answered, "But... I don't have much time." The teacher said, "How about a smoothie? A smoothie is very healthy!"

That night, Yayoi asked her mother to teach her *how to make a smoothie. She learned how to make a smoothie and drank one every morning. After ③ <u>that</u>, she has never felt sick and she studied a lot in class in the morning. She understood that it is important for her to eat breakfast every morning.

（注） *In short　つまり　　*affect　～に影響する　　*school performance　学業
*how to make a smoothie　スムージーの作り方

(1) ①(get) を本文中に適した形に直しなさい。

よく出る！ 動詞の活用 直前の語句に注目しよう！

→直前のatに注目しよう。atは前置詞であり，後ろには名詞が必要なので，動詞のgetは動名詞のgettingになる。

→名詞的用法の不定詞（to＋動詞の原形）は前置詞の後ろに置けないので注意しておこう。

＋plus α 覚えておくべき他の動詞の活用パターン

①be動詞の後 → ～ing ＝ 進行形 / → 過去分詞 ＝ 受動態

②haveの後 → 過去分詞 ＝ 現在完了

(2) 下線部② themが指すものを本文中の英語で答えなさい。

よく出る！ 代名詞の内容（名詞を指す場合） 前にある名詞を探そう！

→代名詞は「すでに出た名詞」の代わりに使われていることが多い。themの場合，複数形の名詞を文章の前の部分から探そう。

→2行前にあるsandwiches（サンドイッチ）をthemにあてはめて訳すと「彼女は朝，朝食を食べる時間がない。だから彼女は学校にサンドイッチを持って行く」となり，意味が通じる。

...from her house by train. Her mother makes sandwiches for her breakfast every morning, but she is not good at ①(get) up early and she has no time to eat breakfast in the morning. So she brings ②them to school.

(3) 下線部③ thatが指す内容を次のア～エから選び記号で答えなさい。

ア teaching Yayoi how to make a smoothie　イ going to the nurse's room

ウ eating sandwiches during lunch time　エ drinking a smoothie in the breakfast

よく出る！ 代名詞の内容（名詞以外を指す場合） 文や文の一部に注目しよう！

→下線部を含む文は「そのあと，彼女は決して気分が悪くなることはなく，午前中の授業でよく勉強した」という意味。直前の文を見ると「彼女はスムージーの作り方を習い，それを毎朝飲んだ」とある。よって，エの「朝食にスムージーを飲むこと」が正解となる。

→この問題では，代名詞がすでに出た「文や文の一部」を指していることに注目しよう。

That night, Yayoi asked her mother to teach her *how to make a smoothie. She learned how to make a smoothie and drank one every morning. After ③that...

【答】 (1) getting　(2) sandwiches　(3) エ

例題2 長い英文を読む練習をしよう

回 次の英文を読んで，あとの問いに答えなさい。 （山口県）

Masato and Tom are junior high school students. They have been friends for a year and Tom has learned how to speak Japanese well during his stay in Japan.

Tom is interested in Japanese culture, especially *manga*. Masato also likes it and they often enjoy talking about the stories. Tom is also interested in *kendo*. He often practices it with Masato. They have had a great time together. But Tom is going to leave Japan and go back to London this July.

On Saturday in June, Masato and Tom went to school to practice *kendo*. After they finished practicing *kendo*, they talked about their homework. It was still difficult for Tom to do homework for Japanese classes alone, so they often did it together and Masato helped Tom. The homework for the weekend was to make *tanka*. They learned about *tanka* in a Japanese class. Tom said, "I don't know how to make *tanka* well. Show me your *tanka* first, please!" Masato said, "I wish I could show you a good one, but making *tanka* is also not easy for me."

Then, Ms. Oka, the teacher of *kendo*, came to them and said, "Are you talking about *tanka*?" Masato remembered that Ms. Oka loved making *tanka*. Masato sometimes saw her good *tanka* in the school newspaper. Masato said, "Yes. We're trying to make *tanka*, but we have no idea. Could you tell us how to make it? It's our homework!" Ms. Oka smiled and said, "OK. Making *tanka* is not so difficult. You can make *tanka* freely." "Freely? But *tanka* has a rule about rhythm," Masato said. She said, "Of course it has some rules. But I think the most important thing is to make *tanka* freely with the words born from your heart. Talk with your heart. Then, you can make good *tanka*."

Masato repeated Ms. Oka's words in his heart and remembered the days with Tom. He thought, "We have enjoyed many things. Saying good-bye to Tom will be sad. But we have to grow in each place for our future. It may be hard but I believe we can." Masato decided to make *tanka* about this feeling and send it to Tom. He thought it would be a good present.

When Masato and Tom left school, Masato looked up at the sky. It was so blue. They stopped and looked at it for a while together. Then, Masato started making his first *tanka* for Tom.

（注） rhythm リズム（ここでは短歌の 5-7-5-7-7 のリズムのこと） heart 心
good-bye さようなら present 贈り物 for a while しばらくの間

⑴　次の質問に対する答えとして，本文の内容に合う最も適切なものを，次のア～エから選び，記号で答えなさい。

（質問）　Why did Masato and Tom often do homework for Japanese classes together?

ア　Because Tom needed Masato's help to do it.

イ　Because Masato was interested in teaching.

ウ　Because Tom liked Japanese classes very much.

エ　Because making *tanka* was easy for Masato.

よく出る！　英問英答　**問題文･選択肢も本文と同じように時間をかけて読もう！**

（質問）なぜマサトとトムはしばしば一緒に日本語の授業の宿題をしていたのか？
ア　トムがそれをするためにマサトの助けが必要だったから。
イ　マサトは教えることに興味があったから。
ウ　トムは国語の授業がとても好きだったから。
エ　マサトにとって短歌を作ることは簡単だったから。

→第3段落の3文目に注目。It was still difficult for Tom to do homework for Japanese classes alone, so they often did it together and Masato helped Tom.（トムにとって1人で国語の授業の宿題をすることはまだ難しかったので，彼らはよくそれを一緒にし，マサトはトムを手伝った）とあるので，アが正解となる。

⑵　次は，本文の内容についての【質問】である。この【質問】に対する適切な答えとなるように，【答え】の下線部に適切な英語4語を書きなさい。

【質問】　According to Ms. Oka, what should Masato do to make good *tanka*?

【答え】　He should ＿＿ and make *tanka* freely.

差がつく!!　内容理解＋英作文　**本文から答えを探そう！**

→質問は「オカ先生によると，よい短歌を作るためにマサトは何をするべきか？」という意味である。オカ先生とマサトが短歌について話している第4段落を見よう。

→オカ先生の最後のせりふに"Talk with your heart"という4語の表現があり，「あなたの心と話し，短歌を自由に作りなさい」という答えが予想できる。

→最後に，主語のHeに合わせてyourをhisに変えることを忘れないようにしよう。

まず【質問】の文からどの段落を見るべきか考えよう！

【答】　⑴ ア　⑵（例）talk with his heart

例題3　よく出るテーマの長文を読もう

□　次の英文を読み，あとの問いに答えなさい。（関大第一高）

All *human beings can learn language. And all human babies learn language the same way. It doesn't *matter what language they are learning. (A) babies can learn any language, but they learn the language they hear around them.

All babies make only one kind of sound at first: crying. In little babies, crying has a purpose. It calls the parents and tells them about a problem. [ア] That's the first kind of conversation babies have with their parents. Soon babies begin making other, happier sounds. These sounds make parents want to stay close and talk to them more. This is how babies begin to learn language — by listening to their parents.

*By the time they are two months old, babies can tell the difference between human voices and other sounds. They can also recognize their mother's voice. In the next few months, their listening skills improve some more. They begin to recognize different spoken sounds. (B) they can hear the difference between "pa" and "ba".

When they are about six months old, babies begin "babbling". This means that they make sounds like "mamama" or "bababa". The babies aren't trying to communicate with these sounds. [イ] In fact, babies often babble when they are alone. These babbling sounds are the same for all babies in the beginning. But soon babies begin to practice mostly the sounds they hear around them.

Children start using words when they are about one year old. (C) they use just one word *at a time. They often say the word and do something at the same time to explain their meaning better. For example, a child may say, "Up!" and *hold out her hands. The parents understand that she wants them to pick her up.

When they are about 18 to 24 months old, children begin using two-word *sentences, such as "Train coming" or "New shoes". [ウ] These sentences become longer in the next few years, but they may not be complete. There may also be some *grammatical mistakes.

By the time they are five or six, most children know a lot of words and can speak in complete sentences. They may still make some mistakes, but now they are ready for the other two skills in language learning: reading and writing.

（注）*human being　人間　　*matter　問題である　　*by the time　〜になる頃に
*at a time　一度に　　*hold out　〜を差し出す　　*sentence　文　　*grammatical　文法的な

(1)　(A)〜(C)に入る適切な語句を次のア〜ウから選びなさい。ただし，同じ記号をくり返し使ってはいけません。

ア　For example　　イ　At first　　ウ　In fact

差がつく!!　語句挿入（文と文をつなぐ語句） 前後のつながりを意識しよう！

A：どんな言葉を赤ちゃんが学んでいるかは問題ではない ⇒ 実際に ⇒ 彼らはどんな言語でも学べるが自分のまわりで耳にする言語を学ぶ

B：赤ちゃんはさまざまな話された音を認識し始める ⇒ 例えば ⇒ 彼らは「パ」と「バ」の違いを聞き分ける

C：子どもは１歳頃に単語を使い始める ⇒ まず ⇒ 彼らは一度に１語だけ使う

＋plus α よく出る文と文をつなぐ語句

for example（例えば）　in fact（実際に）　at first（まず）　at last（ついに）
however（しかし）　as a result（結果として）　instead（その代わりに）

(2)　以下の二つの英文を入れるのに正しい位置を文中の ア ～ ウ から選びなさい。

① They're just trying out sounds and learning how to use their mouths.

② They may be hungry, afraid, or hurt.

差がつく!!　文挿入 まずは予想し，そのあと確認をしよう

予想 ①：just trying out sounds（ただ音を出そうとする）に注目

⇒ イ の前にある"mamama"や"bababa"という音に関係があるのではないか？

②：hungry, afraid, or hurt（空腹であるか，怖いのか，あるいは痛いのか）に注目

⇒ ア の前にあるa problem（問題）の具体例ではないか？

確認 ①「赤ちゃんはこれらの音でコミュニケーションを図ろうとしているのではありません。彼らはただ音を出そうとしたり，口の使い方を学んだりしているのです」

②「小さな赤ちゃんのとき，泣くことには目的があります。それは親を呼び，彼らに問題について伝えます。彼らは空腹であるか，怖いか，あるいは痛いのかもしれません」

(3)　この文章につける題名として最も適切なものを次のア～エから選びなさい。

ア　How Babies Communicate with Parents　　イ　How Human Beings Learn English

ウ　How Children Learn Language　　エ　The Best Way of Learning English

差がつく!!　題名選択 本文のテーマとあっているかが最重要！

ア「どうやって赤ちゃんは両親とコミュニケーションをとるか」
イ「どうやって人間は英語を学ぶか」
ウ「どうやって子どもは言葉を学ぶか」
エ「英語を学ぶ一番よい方法」

「両親とのコミュニケーション」「英語を学ぶ」はテーマではない

→第2段落以降で「成長するにつれて子どもがどのように言葉を身につけていくのか」が説明されている。よって本文のテーマは「子どもの言葉の習得」であり，ウと一致する。

【答】 (1) A. ウ　B. ア　C. イ　(2) ① イ　② ア　(3) ウ

☆次のページからのStep upでは，入試でよく出るテーマの長文問題に取り組もう！

STEP UP

1　次の英文を読んで，各問いに答えなさい。（テーマ：物語）　　　　　　　　　　　　　（昇陽高）

Toby loved animals. He had two dogs and a cat at home, and he also wanted to get a bird. His mom told him (あ)<u>he had enough pets so he couldn't keep any more pets</u>.

One day Toby was on his way to the movies and (i)<u>see</u> a *kitten under a tree.

"What's wrong?" Toby asked the kitten. "Did someone forget to take you home?" The kitten looked very young and very afraid. (い)<u>Toby decided to give up the movies</u> and bring the kitten to his house. "Toby, what do you have there?" Mom asked. "I found (A)<u>him</u> under a tree on *Willow Street," said Toby. "He doesn't have any *tags so I thought I should bring him home." "You already have enough pets, Toby." "But Mom, (う)<u>(him / leave / couldn't / there / I)</u>." Mom gave the kitten some milk and something to eat.

The next day, Toby was on his way home from school and found another kitten! "Oh, are you (ii)<u>lose</u> too?" Toby took that kitten home too. "Toby, you cannot keep these two kittens!" said Mom. "We will take them to the *shelter, so someone else can give (B)<u>them</u> a good home." Toby was sad that he could not keep the kittens.

Toby and his mom took the kittens to the shelter the next day. An officer of the shelter welcomed them.

Just then, a little girl and her mom (iii)<u>come</u> into the shelter and found the kittens. "Mom, look, the kittens are over there!" The little girl (iv)<u>run</u> to the kittens. "Those are my kittens!" cried the girl. Her mom said that maybe they got out through the small hole in the wall. Toby said to the girl, "I found them on Willow Street, and took them home to take care of them."

"We are so glad (C)<u>you</u> found them," said the girl's mother. Toby (v)<u>feel</u> so much better to know that the kittens were going to be safe and in a good home. "We have to repair the wall" said the girl's mother. "We don't want (D)<u>them</u> to get out again."

They both thanked Toby and his mom for the care (E)<u>they</u> gave the kittens. She picked up one of them. The girl said (え)<u>"I'm going to name it Toby</u>." Toby smiled and said he would visit the kittens. "You are always welcome," said the girl's mom. Toby gave the kittens a smile and said good-bye.

注　*kitten　子猫　　*Willow Street　柳通り（通りの名称）　　*tag　名札　　*shelter　保護施設

(1)　下線部(i)～(v)の動詞について，前後関係から最も適切な形をア～エの中から１つずつ選びなさい。

(i)　ア　see　　イ　saw　　ウ　seen　　エ　seeing

(ii)　ア　lost　　イ　lose　　ウ　loss　　エ　losing

(iii) ア cume　イ come　ウ comed　エ came

(iv) ア ranned　イ runned　ウ ran　エ run

(v) ア feel　イ felt　ウ fell　エ feeling

(2) 下線部(A)～(E)の代名詞が示すものをア～エの中から1つずつ選びなさい。

(A) ア Toby　イ a kitten　ウ a dog　エ his friend

(B) ア someone　イ his birds　ウ dogs　エ kittens

(C) ア Toby　イ Toby's mother　ウ an officer　エ a little girl

(D) ア Toby and his mother　イ a girl and her mother　ウ kittens　エ dogs

(E) ア Toby and his mother　イ a girl and her mother　ウ kittens　エ Toby

(3) 次の①～⑤の日本文が本文の内容と合っていれば○を，間違っていれば×を選びなさい。

① トビーは，犬と鳥を飼っていた。

② トビーは映画を観に行く途中で猫を見つけた。

③ トビーは通りで見つけた猫に，自分で餌を運んであげた。

④ トビーの見つけた猫は飼い主が捨てた猫だった。

⑤ 猫の飼い主は，トビーがこれからも猫に会いに来るのを許してくれた。

(4) 下線部(あ)の英文の意味として最も適切なものを，ア～エの中から1つ選びなさい。

ア 彼は十分な数のペットを飼っていたけれど，そのほかのペットも飼えた。

イ 彼はもうこれ以上ペットが飼えなくなるほどはペットを飼っていなかった。

ウ 彼はペットを飼っていなかった。そこでこれ以上飼うことができなかった。

エ 彼は十分な数のペットを飼っていた。だからもうこれ以上ペットは飼えなかった。

(5) 下線部(い)の理由を日本語で答えなさい。

(6) 下線部(う)「僕はその猫をそこに放っておけなかった」という意味になるように，(　　)内の語句を並べ替えなさい。

(7) 下線部(え)を日本語にしなさい。

1	(1)	(i)		(ii)		(iii)		(iv)		(v)	
	(2)	(A)		(B)		(C)		(D)		(E)	
	(3)	①		②		③		④		⑤	
	(4)										
	(5)										
	(6)										
	(7)										

2 環境活動家グレタ・トゥンベリさん（Greta Thunberg）に関する英文を読み，以下の問いに答えなさい。なお，グレタさんのスピーチ（原文）は平易なものに書きかえています。（テーマ：人物）

（大阪暁光高）

Greta Thunberg was born（ ① ）*Sweden in 2003. When she was eight years old, she first heard about climate change. She was ② (tell) to turn off the lights to save energy and to recycle paper. At school she was ③ (shock) to see the movie of waste in the sea. She got angry with adults who did nothing for stopping the global warming. When she was fifteen years old, she decided not to go to school and to sit on the ground in front of the *Parliament every day by herself. She had a sign that said, "School *Strike for Climate. ④ Do not Destroy our Future." Her voice quickly ⑤ (draw) attentions. A lot of young people began to sit and strike all over the world on Fridays. This great *movement is now called "Fridays for Future."

Greta spoke up because ⑥ (to / wanted / she / people / know) that there is a problem in our world. "My name is Grata Thunberg. I am fifteen years old and I'm（ ⑦ ）Sweden. Many people say that Sweden is a very small country, but I've learned that no one is too small to make a difference. When I started School Strike, some people said that I should be in school and study. But we can't save the world by playing by the rules. Everything needs to be changed," she said in 2018. One year later at the UN, she made a speech. "I should be back in school. You have taken my dreams away. But I'm one of the lucky ones. People are suffering. People are dying. Whole *ecosystems are falling down. We are in the beginning of a *mass extinction. But you always talk about only money. *How dare you!" Greta was *nominated for Nobel Peace Prize in 2019.

If there is anything wrong, you can raise your voice. You can use the Internet, or talk with your friends and family, or write letters to Parliament. ⑧ Your voice has the power to change the world. Your future is in your hands.

（注） Sweden：スウェーデン　Parliament：国会　strike：ストライキ　movement：運動
ecosystem：生態系　mass extinction：大量絶滅　How dare you!：よくもそんなことを！
nominate：ノミネートする

(1) （ ① ）（ ⑦ ）に入る適切な英語を次から選び記号で答えなさい。

ア at　イ from　ウ in

(2) 下線部②③⑤の（　）内の英語を適切な形に変えなさい。

(3) 下線部④⑧を日本語にしなさい。

(4) 下線部⑥を意味が通るように正しく並べかえなさい。

(5) 次の文を読み，本文の内容と一致するものには○を，違うものには×をつけなさい。

① グレタさんは15歳から気候変動に関する運動を始めた。

② グレタさんは毎日学校を休み，一人で国会の前に座り込んだ。

③ 世界中の若者たちも，グレタさんと共に運動に参加するようになった。

④ 2018年にグレタさんは国連でスピーチをした。

⑤ スウェーデンは小さい国なので，何も変化を起こすことはできないとグレタさんは思っている。

(6) 次の文を読み，グレタさんの主張と合っているものを２つ選び記号で答えなさい。

ア Following the rules can't save the world.

イ "School Strike for Climate" is the only way to solve the problems.

ウ Everything in school should not be changed.

エ Leaders of the world always talk about money.

(7) 本文の内容と一致するように，次の応答を完成させなさい。

① Why did Greta get angry?

—Because (　　) did nothing for stopping the (　　) (　　).

② What is Greta's movement called?

—It is called (　　) (　　) (　　).

2											
	(1)	①		⑦							
	(2)	②		③		⑤					
	(3)	④									
		⑧									
	(4)										
	(5)	①		②		③		④		⑤	
	(6)										
	(7)	①	Because (　　) did nothing for stopping the (　　)(　　).								
		②	It is called (　　)(　　)(　　).								

3　次の英語スピーチを読んで，後の各問いに答えなさい。（テーマ:文化）　（神戸星城高）

Hello, everyone. I am Sachiko. I chose "(㋐)" for today's topic. Before I begin my speech, ㋑(あなた方に１つ質問がしたいです). Do you like looking at paintings? You may think that ㋒ it is difficult to understand them. In fact, I thought so too when I first visited an art museum. However, the other day, my art teacher ㋓(ア give　イ gave　ウ given) me three hints to enjoy it. Let me introduce them to you.

First, try to find some symbols such as flowers, animals, or clothes in the painting. When you find them, try to think of the meaning behind them. You can find famous characters easily by learning the meanings of symbols. (㋔), the color blue is the symbol of Maria, the mother of Jesus, so she often wears blue clothes. If you know this rule, it will be easy to find her in a painting. (㋕), in the pictures of Greek and Roman myths, Apollo, a god of the Sun, is usually playing music and wears a crown made of leaves. Learn the rules of symbols, (㋖) it will be fun to see your favorite characters in paintings.

Second, you will enjoy paintings more if you know about the compositions. The triangle composition is the most common. In this composition, the main characters are in the middle of the picture, and they shape triangle. When you see this shape, you will feel easy and comfortable. (㋗), the triangle composition is used in peaceful paintings.

Finally, and most importantly, be honest with your emotions when you look at the paintings. When you see a picture you like, ask yourself, "Why do I like this?" and tell the reasons to others. ㋘(ア Some　イ Any　ウ Many) reason is all right, so think freely. Next time, you can find your favorite paintings more easily.

If you know what to look for in a painting, you will enjoy looking at paintings more. Think about the points above when you visit an art museum. The paintings may look more ㋙(ア interest　イ interested　ウ interesting) to you.

【注】 painting　絵画　Jesus　イエス・キリスト
Greek and Roman myths　ギリシア・ローマ神話　crown　かんむり　composition　構図
shape ～　～の形を作る

(1) ㋐に入る語として最も適切なものを下から選び，その記号で答えなさい。

ア math　イ Japanese　ウ English　エ art　オ science

(2) ㋑の日本語を表す英文になるよう，(　　) 内に入る英語を１語ずつ答えなさい。

I'd (　　) (　　) ask (　　) a question.

(3) 下線部㋒を，"them" が何を指すのかを明らかにしながら日本語にしなさい。

(4) ㋓㋙に入る語を (　　) 内からそれぞれ１つずつ選び，その記号で答えなさい。

(5) ㋔㋕㋗に入る語句を下から選び，その記号で答えなさい。

ア Also　イ In this way　ウ For this reason　エ For example

(6) ㋖にあてはまる接続詞として最も適切なものを下から選び，その記号で答えなさい。

ア and　イ or　ウ but

(7)　意味が通る英文になるように，㋘の（　　）内から適切な語を選び，その記号で答えなさい。

(8)　文中の “the triangle composition” の効果として最も適切なものを下から選び，その記号で答えなさい。

ア　鑑賞者の悲しみが大きくなる。

イ　鑑賞者に安心感を与える。

ウ　鑑賞者を不安定な気持ちにさせる。

(9)　文中の “the triangle composition” が使われている絵を１つ選び，その記号で答えなさい。

ア

イ

ウ

(10)　本文の内容を踏まえ，右の絵の中からアポロ神を選び，その記号で答えなさい。

(11)　本文の内容と一致するものを，ア～オから２つ選び，その記号で答えなさい。

ア　絵画を楽しむには，花や動物の生態について知る必要がある。

イ　描かれる象徴のルールを知っていると，絵画に登場する人物が誰なのかがわかる。

ウ　絵画の構図などの基本的な情報は，絵画をより楽しむこととは無関係である。

エ　絵画を楽しむうえで最も大切なのは，気に入った絵画に出会ったら，なぜ好きなのだろうと自問自答し，その理由を誰かに言ってみることである。

オ　絵画を楽しむコツは，「象徴を見つけること」「絵画の基本的な情報を知っていること」「好きな絵画だけを見ること」である。

3										
	(1)		(2)	I'd (　　) (　　) ask (　　) a question.						
	(3)									
	(4)	㋓		㋙		(5) ㋔		㋕		㋗
	(6)		(7)		(8)		(9)		(10)	
	(11)									

4　次の英文を読み，各問いに答えなさい。（テーマ：生物・生命）　　（四天王寺東高）

*Manatees

Manatees are large, slow, peaceful animals that only live in a few places in the world. They can live for forty years and grow to 600 kilograms. There are 3 kinds of manatees; they live in parts of the United States, South America, and Africa. Manatees live quiet lives. They often swim alone. If you see a group of manatees together, it will probably ① (be) small (less than six members). They usually swim slowly, about 8 kilometers an hour. They can reach speeds of 24 kilometers an hour, but can only swim that fast for a very short time.

Manatees are *mammals. When the babies are young, they drink milk from their mothers. But they are different from other mammals in an interesting way. Most mammals, including dogs, cats, humans, and giraffes, have seven *bones in their necks. Manatees only have six. (A) <u>This</u> means they cannot turn their heads to see behind them. They have to slowly turn their whole bodies. Manatees' eyes are small, but they can see very well. However, because of their different necks, they can only see things that are in front of them.

One of the best places to see manatees is in *Florida, a place with beautiful nature in the United States.

In the 1970s, there ② (be) only a few hundred manatees in Florida. Many people were (B) that soon all the manatees would die. They worked hard to clean the manatees' rivers and made laws to protect them from boats in the summer. Since then, the number has increased and now there are more than 6 thousand. However, now in 2021, manatees are again *in danger. There have ③ (be) more deaths in the first half of this year than in all of 2020.

The reason more manatees are dying this year is that there isn't enough food for them to eat. A healthy manatee should eat about 10% of its *weight every day. In winter, manatees eat the grass that grows at the *bottom of rivers in Florida. Recently, because more people live in Florida, the water in these places has become dirty with pollution. Light from the sun can't reach the bottom of the rivers and it has been hard for the grass to grow.

In summer, the water becomes warmer and manatees move to the ocean. There, they can find more space and more food. So, at this moment, they don't have to worry about that. But in summer there ④ (be) another problem: The ocean around Florida is a popular place for people to enjoy using boats and doing water sports. The boats these people use go very fast and it is difficult to find the gray manatees as they swim near the top of the water. (C) <u>Every summer many manatees die in boat accidents.</u>

The problem in Florida is very serious. If the number of manatees in Florida continues to go down, it will be very difficult to improve the situation. Manatees usually only have one baby at a time and mother manatees are often *pregnant for twelve months before their babies are born. For this reason, we have ⑤ (be) very careful and continue to check the number of manatees in Florida.

注 *manatee　マナティー（海に住む哺乳動物の１つ）　*mammal　哺乳動物
*bone　骨　*Florida　フロリダ州（アメリカ南東部の州）　*in danger　危機にある
*weight　体重　*bottom　底　*pregnant　妊娠している

(1)　①～⑤の be 動詞の形として適切なものを選び，記号で答えなさい。

①　ア　be　イ　being　ウ　been　エ　to be
②　ア　are　イ　is　ウ　was　エ　were
③　ア　be　イ　being　ウ　been　エ　to be
④　ア　are　イ　is　ウ　was　エ　were
⑤　ア　be　イ　are　ウ　being　エ　to be

(2)　下線部(A)の this はどのようなことをさしているか。記号で答えなさい。

ア　マナティーが子供をミルクで育てること。
イ　マナティーの首の骨の数が他の動物よりも少ないこと。
ウ　マナティーが後ろを振り向くことができないこと。
エ　マナティーが自分の前のものしか見ることができないこと。

(3)　文脈を考えて，空欄（ B ）に入る語を次の中から選び，記号で答えなさい。

ア　excited　イ　surprised　ウ　worried　エ　tired

(4)　下線部(C)に関して，なぜ毎年夏にボートの事故で死んでしまうマナティーが多いのか。原因の１つについて空欄を適切な日本語で埋めなさい。

水面近くを泳ぐ灰色のマナティーが（　　）から。

(5)　本文の内容にあてはまる記述を以下の中から３つ選びなさい。

ア　Manatees usually swim in large groups.
イ　Manatees can swim fast for a long time without getting tired.
ウ　After the 1970s, the number of manatees increased.
エ　Manatees often eat fish.
オ　Water pollution is one reason for manatees' deaths.
カ　Manatees live in the ocean in the winter.
キ　It is very difficult for people in Florida to increase the number of manatees.

4	(1)	①		②		③		④		⑤	
	(2)		(3)								
	(4)	水面近くを泳ぐ灰色のマナティーが									から。
	(5)										

5 次は，中学生の友紀（Yuki）が，いとこの聡史（Satoshi）が泊まりにきた時の体験について，英語の授業でスピーチをしたものである。英文を読んで，(1)～(5)の問いに答えなさい。

（テーマ:体験スピーチ）（熊本県）

Today, I want to talk about my experience during winter vacation. Last December, my aunt and uncle stayed at my house for three days, and I met their son, Satoshi, for the first time. He is only two years old. It was a good chance for me to learn how to take care of little children like him [①] I want to be a nursery school teacher in the future.

On the first day, we went to a zoo and saw many animals. I held his hand and walked with him, but sometimes I walked too [②] for him. He often cried and asked me to stop. Walking slowly with little children was a little difficult for me, but I found that it is important when I take care of them.

On the second day, we enjoyed singing songs and playing with a ball in my house all day long. When we were playing together, he talked to me a lot, but I couldn't understand some of his words. When I tried hard to listen to his words, he smiled and talked to me more. I learned that listening carefully is important for communication with little children.

On the last day, we ate lunch together. Satoshi couldn't use his spoon well and kept spilling his food on the table. So, I took his spoon away from his hand and brought the food to his mouth with it. I thought I did a good thing, but my aunt looked sad and asked me to stop. She said, "Yuki, thank you for helping Satoshi like his older sister, but he is trying to do his best. He is learning now, so, just [③] him." I learned that helping too much is not good for little children when they are trying to do something.

During his stay, I had a lot of good experiences. I learned that it is important for us to have many experiences and to make many mistakes. Through mistakes, we can learn [　]. I learned important things from Satoshi.

（注）nursery school teacher＝保育士　all day long－一日中　carefully－注意深く
spoon＝スプーン　spill ～＝～をこぼす　take ～ away＝～を取り上げる
make a mistake＝失敗する

(1) [①]～[③] に入れるのに最も適当なものを，それぞれ次のア～ウから１つ選び，記号で答えなさい。

[①]　ア because　イ but　ウ or

[②]　ア easily　イ straight　ウ fast

[③]　ア ask　イ stop　ウ watch

(2) 本文の内容について，次の質問に英語で答えなさい。

Where were Yuki and Satoshi on the second day?

(3) [　] に入れるのに最も適当なものを，次のア～ウから１つ選び，記号で答えなさい。

ア how to ask meanings of some words　イ how to do things better

ウ how to sing songs

(4) 次の「翔太(しょうた)のメモ」は，クラスメートの翔太が，友紀のスピーチを聞いてその内容を書きとめたものである。本文の内容に合うように，［A］～［C］にそれぞれ適当なことばを日本語で書きなさい。

「翔太のメモ」

友紀が聡史との体験を通して学んだこと
〈1日目〉　幼い子どもと一緒のときには，［A］ことが大事だということ。
〈2日目〉　幼い子どもとのコミュニケーションでは，しっかりと［B］ことが大事だということ。
〈3日目〉　幼い子どもが何かをやろうとしているときには，［C］ことはよくないということ。

(5) 本文の内容に合っているものを，次のア～ウから1つ選び，記号で答えなさい。

ア　It was the second time for Yuki to meet Satoshi last December.

イ　When Yuki helped Satoshi with eating lunch, Yuki's aunt looked very happy.

ウ　Yuki had many good experiences with Satoshi during the winter vacation.

5	(1)	①		②		③	
	(2)						
	(3)						
	(4)	A		B		C	
	(5)						

6 次の英文を読んで，問いに答えなさい。 テーマ:環境・エネルギー （好文学園女高）

Have you ever heard of the word, "plastic rain?" When scientists researched the rain, they found very small pieces of plastic in the rainwater. They were found in 90% of the rain. People in the world were surprised to hear the report and they became interested in the problem. These very small pieces of plastic are called "microplastics." Microplastics are produced from so many plastic products around us. For example, we often see marine debris on beaches and in the sea. Some of them are plastic bottles and plastic bags. They do not return to the nature and are broken down by the sun's light into smaller pieces. (あ), now there are so many microplastics on beaches and in the sea.

So why are there microplastics in the rain? They are not only in the sea but (1) in the air! For example, synthetic fibers used for our clothes are also plastic products and they can easily become microplastics. ①<u>This kind of microplastics is too small to see with our own eyes</u>. They are carried by the wind and fall to the ground around the world with the rain or the snow. They were found even in the Arctic.

(2) microplastics are very small, they may produce big problems in the future. Fish in the sea may keep eating microplastics. We may keep eating the fish without knowing ②<u>that</u>. We may keep breathing in so many microplastics in the air. We must be careful that microplastics don't enter our bodies. (い), even scientists don't know how microplastics influence our health.

The environmental problems with plastic are becoming more serious. So many companies in the world have started to think about how they solve ③<u>them</u>. Some supermarkets and convenience stores stop giving plastic bags for free. Some coffee shops and fast-food restaurants stop using plastic straws and start using paper straws.

Now ④<u>we must do something to stop plastic pollution</u>. ⑤<u>(we / there / two / right / can / are / do / things) away</u>. First, let's pick up plastic trash in the neighborhood. It often goes into the river and finally reaches the sea. If we clean the streets near us, we can clean the sea far from us. Second, let's reduce the use of plastic products such as plastic bottles and plastic bags. (う), shall we bring our own water bottles and shopping bags? It may be difficult (3) just one person to stop the pollution by doing these things. However, if people in the world do them all together, we can ⑥<u>do it</u>. Then we may be able to see the future without plastic rain.

注）marine debris 漂流ごみ・漂着ごみ　synthetic fiber 合成繊維　the Arctic 北極
breathe in 吸い込む　influence 影響を及ぼす

(1) (あ)～(う)の中に入る最も適切なものをそれぞれア～エの中から１つずつ選び，記号で答えなさい。

ア As a result　イ By the way　ウ However　エ Instead

(2) （ 1 ）～（ 3 ）の中に入る最も適切なものをそれぞれア～エの中から1つずつ選び，記号で答えなさい。

1　ア such　イ also　ウ as　エ so

2　ア Until　イ With　ウ That　エ Though

3　ア of　イ from　ウ for　エ with

(3) 下線部①の英文を下記のように書き換えたとき（ A ）（ B ）に入る適切な語の組み合わせを下から1つ選び，記号で答えなさい。

This kind of microplastics is（ A ）small that we（ B ）see them with our own eyes.

ア A very B can　イ A very B cannot　ウ A so B can

エ A so B cannot

(4) 下線部② that，⑥ do it が指す内容をそれぞれ日本語で答えなさい。

(5) 下線部③ them が指している内容を，本文中より五語で抜き出しなさい。

(6) 下線部④を日本語に訳しなさい。

(7) 下線部⑤の（　　）内の語を本文の内容に合うように並べ換えなさい。ただし，文の始めに来る語も小文字にしてあります。

(8) 次のア～カの中から本文の内容に合っているものを2つ選び，記号で答えなさい。

ア Scientists discovered microplastics in the rain they checked out.

イ The sun's light breaks down plastics into smaller pieces and they go back to the nature.

ウ Synthetic fiber is good for our clothes but becomes microplastics easily in the Arctic.

エ Only scientists can find the influence of microplastics in the future.

オ Some supermarkets and convenience stores are free to give chopsticks.

カ If people in the world clean the streets and use their own water bottles and shopping bags, plastic rain may stop in the future.

6									
	(1)	あ		い		う			
	(2)	1		2		3		(3)	
	(4)	②							
		⑥							
	(5)								
	(6)								
	(7)								away.
	(8)								

7 次の英文を読んで，後の問いに答えなさい。 テーマ:社会·時事問題 （関西大学北陽高）

Dr. Drew Pate is an *expert on *teenagers. He helps teenagers who feel sad or *worried. He also speaks with their parents. When he talks to them, ①one thing *comes up all the time. People are worried about websites like Instagram, Facebook or Snapchat. Such websites are called social media. People can connect with others through messages and *posts. 【 A 】 Parents *wonder if they are bad for teenagers.

Scientists are trying to find out the effect of social media on teenagers. ②Some studies have shown that using social media has a bad effect on some young people. It can make them worried and *depressed. 【 B 】 When people are depressed, they have trouble feeling happy. They may not be able to control their *mood. They may have trouble sleeping.

(③), some scientists say that using social media can also help teenagers. 【 C 】 For example, one study looked at teenagers who were playing video games for many hours. Heavy gamers who spent time with friends on social media *seemed to feel less depressed or worried than gamers who ④didn't. Another good point of social media is that ⑤(ア give / イ talk / ウ them / エ it / オ to / カ can / キ a chance) about their problems. In this way, they can be themselves.

Dr. Pate said that using social media causes too many problems for some teenagers. They may need to (⑥) completely. Some teenagers just need to spend less time on the websites. They may also need to communicate with a small group of friends. Other teenagers use social media well. For them, the websites are simply fun. "It's different for every teenager," Dr. Pate said.

【注】 *expert 専門家　*teenagers 10代の若者　*worried 心配している
*comes up 話題に上がる　*posts 投稿　*wonder if ～ ～かどうか疑問に思う
*depressed 気分が落ち込んだ　*mood 気持ち　*seemed ～ ～のようだった

(1) 下線部①が指しているものを本文中から英語2語で抜き出しなさい。

(2) 次の英文は本文から抜き出したものである。この英文が入る最も適切な場所を，文中の【 A 】～【 C 】から1つ選び，記号で答えなさい。

Many parents say that their children are always on social media.

(3) 下線部②を日本語で表すとき，(　　) に入る適切な表現を答えなさい。

「ソーシャルメディアを使うことは (　　) ということを (　　)。」

(4) (③) に入る最も適切なものをア～エから1つ選び，記号で答えなさい。

ア In addition　イ However　ウ Therefore　エ Of course

(5) 下線部④の didn't 以下に省略されているものを英語で答えなさい。

(6) 下線部⑤が「それは彼らに自分たちの問題について話す機会を与えることができる」という意味になるように (　　) 内の語句を並べ替えたとき，(　　) 内で4番目と6番目にくるものをア～キから選び，それぞれ記号で答えなさい。

(7) (⑥) に入る最も適切なものをア～エから1つ選び，記号で答えなさい。

ア give it up　　イ continue it　　ウ put it on　　エ change it

(8) 本文の内容と一致しないものをア～オから２つ選び，記号で答えなさい。

ア Dr. Pate is an expert and helps teenagers who are in trouble.

イ Snapchat is a website loved by old Internet users.

ウ In social media, people can communicate by using messages and posts.

エ Feeling depressed may cause some trouble on teenagers.

オ Dr. Pate said that all teenagers use social media badly.

<table>
<tr><td rowspan="4">7</td><td>(1)</td><td colspan="2"></td><td>(2)</td><td></td></tr>
<tr><td>(3)</td><td colspan="4">ソーシャルメディアを使うことは（　　　　　　　　　　）という
ことを（　　　　　　　　　　）。</td></tr>
<tr><td>(4)</td><td></td><td>(5)</td><td colspan="2">didn’t</td></tr>
<tr><td>(6)</td><td>4番目</td><td>6番目</td><td>(7)</td><td>(8)</td></tr>
</table>

② 英作文

例題1 ◀整序作文▶

回 日本文の意味を表すように，（　　）内の語句を並べかえて英文を完成させなさい。

(1) 将来ダンサーになりたいと思います。（大阪信愛学院高）

(to / I / a dancer / want / in / be / the) future.

(2) 先生は私たちに教室を掃除してほしかった。（賢明学院高）

Our teacher (us / our / wanted / to / classroom / clean).

> **アドバイス**
> 文の中心となる〈主語＋動詞〉をまずは完成させよう！
>
> 例：私は車を持っています。
> ⇒ I（私は(主語)） have（持っている(動詞)） a car.（車を）
>
> 文法ポイント：不定詞　よく出る構文を覚えよう！（※構文＝文のパターン）
>
> (1) 「〜したい」＝ want to do 〜
>
> I（私は） want to be（なりたい） a dancer（ダンサーに） in the future.（将来）
>
> (2) 「Aに〜(することを)してほしい」＝ want A to do
>
> Our teacher（私たちの先生は） wanted（してほしかった） us（私たちに） to clean our classroom.（私たちの教室を掃除することを）

(3) その映画は僕を泣かせました。（滋賀短期大学附高［改題］）

(cry / the / made / movie / me).

> 差がつく文法：原形不定詞
>
> →文の動詞が使役動詞（〜させる）の場合，〈使役動詞＋A＋do(動詞の原形)〉の語順になると，「Aに〜(することを)させる」という意味になる。また，このdoのことを原形不定詞（toがなく，動詞の原形の形をしている不定詞）と呼ぶ。
> →使役動詞にはmake・have・letなどがある。
>
> The movie（その映画は） made（使役動詞／させた） me（僕に） cry.（原形不定詞／泣くことを）

【答】(1) I want to be a dancer in the　(2) wanted us to clean our classroom
(3) The movie made me cry

例題２　◀自由英作文▶

回　次の場面と状況を踏まえ，下の(1)，(2)の問いに答えなさい。　（岩手県）

〔場面〕　あなたは英語の授業で，友人のマーク（Mark）にメッセージを伝える方法について，次のワークシートに自分の考えとその理由を書いています。

〔状況〕　アメリカに帰国した友人のマーク（Mark）が，ある試合に勝利しました。

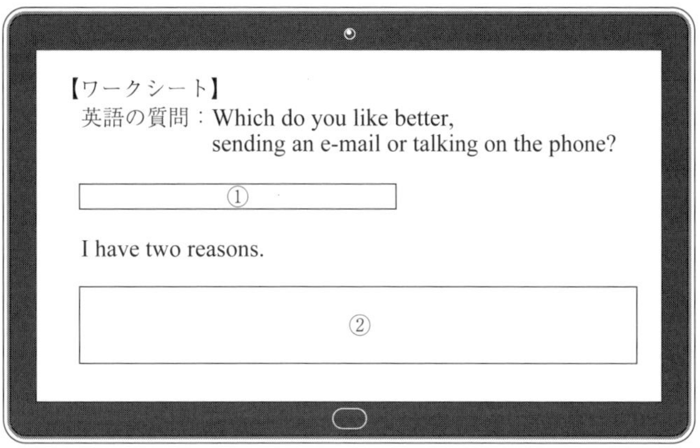

(1)　この〔状況〕で，あなたはどちらの方法を選びますか。ワークシートの英語の質問の答えとして，［　①　］に入る適当な英語を，6語以上で書きなさい。ただし，e-mailは1語として数えます。

(2)　(1)で選んだ理由となるように，［　②　］に入る適当な英語を，20語以上で書きなさい。ただし，文の数はいくつでもかまいません。

アドバイス

・「何を答えなければいけないのか」をまずは把握する。
　→(1)は「メールと電話のどちらを選ぶか」，(2)は「それを選んだ理由」

解答例1	(1)	メールを送ることがより好きだ。
	(2)	電話で話すことはお金がかかり，メールは時間があるときに読める。
解答例2	(1)	電話で話すことがよりよい。
	(2)	メッセージをすぐに伝えることができ，声を聴くことができる。

文法ポイント：比較　**原級・比較級・最上級の活用を覚えよう！**

(1)	語尾にer・estをつける	例：small - smaller - smallest
(2)	前にmore・mostをおく	例：expensive - more expensive - most expensive
(3)	不規則変化	例：good(well) - better - best

【答】（例1）(1) I like sending an e-mail better.（6語）(2) First, I think talking on the phone is more expensive. Second, Mark can read my e-mail when he has time.（20語）

（例2）(1) Talking on the phone is better.（6語）(2) One reason is that I can tell my message quickly. The other reason is that I can hear his voice.（20語）

§ 1．整序作文

1 (1)～(5)が，それぞれ日本語の内容を表す英文になるように（　　）内の語句を並べかえたとき，（　　）内で2番目と4番目に来る語句を記号で答えなさい。ただし，文頭の文字も小文字で示してあります。　　　　　　　　　　　　　　　　　　　　　　　　　（あべの翔学高）

(1) カバンの中に何本ペンを持っていますか。
(ア you　イ many　ウ do　エ how　オ pens) have in your bag?

(2) 明日，彼に電話をかけます。
I (ア will　イ tomorrow　ウ him　エ call).

(3) どちらの絵が彼女のものですか。
(ア hers　イ is　ウ which　エ picture)?

(4) 私はふつう夕食後に音楽を聴きます。
I (ア after　イ dinner　ウ listen　エ usually　オ to music).

(5) タクミの家の前に本屋があります。
There (ア in　イ of　ウ a bookstore　エ front　オ is) Takumi's house.

2 次の日本文の意味を表すように，（　　）内の語を並べかえ，（　　）内で3番目と5番目にくる語の記号を答えなさい。ただし，文頭にくる語も小文字で表示されています。（関西福祉科学大学高）

(1) ここから駅までどれくらいかかりますか。
(ア get　イ from　ウ does　エ how　オ here　カ long　キ to　ク take　ケ it) to the station?

(2) 日曜日に散歩しませんか。
(ア on　イ walk　ウ Sunday　エ a　オ about　カ taking　キ how)?

(3) 京都には観光の名所がたくさんある。
(ア are　イ to　ウ places　エ there　オ many　カ visit) in Kyoto.

(4) 学校へ行く途中に彼女に会った。
I (ア to　イ on　ウ way　エ her　オ school　カ my　キ met).

(5) この歌は世界中で歌われている。
This song (ア world　イ all　ウ is　エ over　オ sung　カ the).

3 日本語に合うように［　　］内の英語を並べかえて，（ A ）に入る語を記号で答えなさい。

（神港学園高）

(1) 郵便局へ行く道を教えてくれませんか。

Can (　　) (　　) (　　) (A) (　　) the post office?

［ア　the way　　イ　you　　ウ　to　　エ　tell　　オ　me］

(2) それはお母さんが私にくれたペンです。

That (　　) (　　) (A) (　　) (　　) me.

［ア　gave　　イ　the pen　　ウ　is　　エ　my mother　　オ　which］

(3) 窓のそばに立っている女性は誰ですか。

Who (　　) the (　　) (　　) (A) (　　)?

［ア　the window　　イ　woman　　ウ　is　　エ　by　　オ　standing］

(4) 私に何か熱い飲み物をください。

Please (　　) (　　) (　　) (A) (　　).

［ア　me　　イ　something　　ウ　give　　エ　to drink　　オ　hot］

(5) 私の兄は２度オーストラリアに行ったことがある。

My brother (　　) (A) (　　) (　　) (　　).

［ア　been　　イ　twice　　ウ　has　　エ　Australia　　オ　to］

(6) トムは忙しすぎて，今あなたを手伝えません。

Tom (　　) (A) (　　) (　　) (　　) now.

［ア　help you　　イ　too　　ウ　to　　エ　busy　　オ　is］

		(1)	(2)	(3)	(4)	(5)
1	2番目					
	4番目					
2		(1)	(2)	(3)	(4)	(5)
	3番目					
	5番目					

3	(1)		(2)		(3)		(4)		(5)		(6)	

4 日本語の意味に合うように（　　）内の語(句)を並べかえたとき，（　　）内で4番目にくる語(句)を記号で答えなさい。ただし，文頭の文字も小文字にしてあります。 （京都明徳高）

(1) どのくらい沖縄に滞在するつもりですか。

How (ア to　イ are　ウ going　エ long　オ you　カ stay) in Okinawa?

(2) あなたはなぜ怒ったのですか？

(ア made　イ angry　ウ what　エ you)?

(3) 私はケンに私と一緒に来てくれるように頼んだ。

I (ア asked　イ me　ウ with　エ Ken　オ to　カ come).

(4) 彼女の考えは私のとは異なります。

(ア different　イ from　ウ is　エ mine　オ her　カ idea).

(5) サッカーの試合はまだ始まっていません。

(ア the soccer game　イ started　ウ has　エ not　オ yet).

(6) 彼女は親切にも私を手伝ってくれた。

She (ア help　イ enough　ウ kind　エ to　オ was　カ me).

5 次の日本文に合うように下の語(句)を並べかえたとき，[　　]に入るものを記号で答えなさい。ただし，文頭にくるべき語も小文字で示してあります。 （大阪偕星学園高）

(1) 私の祖父はたいてい9時に寝ます。

＿＿ ＿＿ [　　] ＿＿ ＿＿ at nine.

ア goes　イ usually　ウ bed　エ to　オ my grandfather

(2) あなたは8時にどこで勉強していたのですか。

＿＿ ＿＿ [　　] ＿＿ ＿＿ eight?

ア were　イ studying　ウ where　エ at　オ you

(3) 彼女は何を言ったらよいかわからなかった。

She ＿＿ ＿＿ [　　] ＿＿ ＿＿.

ア what　イ say　ウ know　エ didn't　オ to

(4) あなたにこの手紙を明日までに彼のところまで届けてもらいたい。

I ＿＿ ＿＿ [A] ＿＿ [B] ＿＿.

ア to him　イ to bring　ウ you　エ this letter　オ want　カ by tomorrow

(5) 木のそばで眠っているネコを見なさい。

Look ＿＿ ＿＿ [C] ＿＿ [D] ＿＿ the tree.

ア is　イ by　ウ sleeping　エ the cat　オ at　カ which

6 次の各文をあとの｛　　｝内の語(句)を使って英文にしたとき，（ A ）と（ B ）に入る最も適当なものをそれぞれ選び，記号で答えなさい。ただし，文頭に来る語も小文字で示しています。

（大谷高）

(1) ケーキのおかわりはいかがですか。

(　　)(　　)(A)(　　)(　　)(B)(　　)(　　)?

｛ア another / イ cake / ウ have / エ like / オ piece of / カ to / キ would / ク you｝

(2) 夜に窓を開けたままにすべきではない。

(　　)(A)(　　)(　　)(　　)(B)(　　)(　　).

｛ア at / イ leave / ウ night / エ not / オ open / カ should / キ the windows / ク you｝

(3) もし私があなたなら，そのようなことを彼女にしないだろう。

If (　　)(A)(　　), (　　)(B)(　　)(　　)(　　) to her.

｛ア a thing / イ do / ウ I / エ I / オ such / カ were / キ wouldn't / ク you｝

(4) 金閣寺は今まで私が訪れたなかで最も美しい寺です。

Kinkaku-ji is (　　)(　　)(A)(　　)(　　)(　　)(B)(　　).

｛ア beautiful / イ ever / ウ I've / エ most / オ temple / カ that / キ the / ク visited｝

(5) 図書館で本を読んでいる少女は私の妹です。

(　　)(A)(　　)(　　)(　　)(B)(　　)(　　).

｛ア a book / イ in / ウ is / エ my / オ reading / カ sister / キ the girl / ク the library｝

(6) どのような音楽に興味がありますか。

(　　)(　　)(A)(　　)(　　)(　　)(B)(　　)?

｛ア are / イ in / ウ interested / エ kind / オ music / カ of / キ what / ク you｝

4	(1)		(2)		(3)		(4)		(5)		(6)	

5	(1)		(2)		(3)					
	(4)	A		B		(5)	C		D	

6		(1)	(2)	(3)	(4)	(5)	(6)
	A						
	B						

7 次の日本文の意味になるように，（　　）内の語（句）を並べかえて英文を完成させなさい。ただし，文頭に来る語も小文字にしてあります。　（報徳学園高）

(1) 両親は午後9時以降私たちにテレビを見せてくれません。
(TV / after / don't / watch / let / us / my parents) 9 p.m.

(2) 明日は今日ほど暑くないでしょう。
(today / tomorrow / as / as / will / hot / be / not).

(3) 私たちは誰の机を運ばなければならないのですか。
(carry / desk / have / whose / do / we / to)?

(4) 彼女が英語の本を読むのは難しくありません。
(English books / difficult / her / not / read / for / to / it's).

(5) あなたはどれくらいの間ずっと数学を勉強しているのですか。
(you / math / long / been / studying / how / have)?

8 次の日本文に合うように，（　　）内の語句を並べかえなさい。ただし文頭にくる語も小文字になっています。　（香ヶ丘リベルテ高）

(1) あなたに会えるのを楽しみにしています。
I am (seeing / forward / looking / to) you.

(2) 私にはこの本を読むのがむずかしい。
(difficult / to read / it / for / is / me) this book.

(3) 私たちは6時まで学校にいた。
We (at / stayed / until / school) six o'clock.

(4) 私たちは食べ物を買うだけの十分なお金を持っていなかった。
We didn't have (enough / buy / food / money / to).

9 次の(1)～(4)の日本文に合うように，（　　）内の語を並べ替えなさい。ただし，文頭に来る語も小文字で書いてあります。　（上宮太子高）

(1) あなたはそれについて心配する必要はありません。
(that / worry / you / have / about / don't / to).

(2) 彼は私たちに辞書を使わないように言いました。
(dictionary / us / he / use / told / a / to / not).

(3) その壊れた椅子をごらんなさい。
(chair / the / at / broken / look).

(4) 私たちを迎えに来てくれた男性は大変親切でした。
(the / who / meet / came / was / to / kind / us / man / very).

§2. 自由英作文

10 次の絵において，①，②の順で対話が成り立つように，①の吹き出しの＿＿に3語以上の英語を書け。 （鹿児島県）

7	(1)	9 p.m.
	(2)	.
	(3)	?
	(4)	.
	(5)	?
8	(1)	I am　　　　you.
	(2)	this book.
	(3)	We　　　　six o'clock.
	(4)	We didn't have　　　　.
9	(1)	.
	(2)	.
	(3)	.
	(4)	.
10		

11 春樹（Haruki）さんと留学生のアン（Ann）さんが話をしています。それぞれの場面に合う会話になるように（　　）内に**3語以上**の英語を書きなさい。なお，対話は①から⑩の順に行われています。

（富山県）

*gym　体育館

*koala　コアラ

12 次の⑴・⑵のイラストの状況を説明する英文を書け。ただし，以下の条件にしたがうこと。

（精華女高）

⑴　条件１　The woman で書き始め，文中に eggs と the supermarket を使用し，これらを含んで全体を 15 語以内の一文で書くこと。

　　条件２　文末は「.」で終わり，符号は語数に含めない。

⑵　条件　（　　）にそれぞれ 4 語以上の英語を入れ，イラストの状況を説明する二文を完成させること。

A girl (　　　) the tree.

Two boys (　　　) the tree.

13 次のイラストの様子を，6語以上の英語で表現しなさい。 （滋賀学園高）

14 次の質問に対するあなた自身の答えを英語で書きなさい。ただし，(1)は3語以上，(2)は4語以上で答えなさい。 （京都精華学園高）

Question：What did you enjoy the best in your junior high school life?

Answer ：(1)［　　　　　］.

Question：Please tell me more.

Answer ：(2)［　　　　　］.

11	②	.
	⑥	The bag is really nice. ?
	⑨	Yes! They were cute. ?
12	(1)	
	(2)	A girl the tree.
		Two boys the tree.
13		
14	(1)	.
	(2)	.

15 次の英文は，彩香（Ayaka）とニック（Nick）との会話である。会話の流れが自然になるように，次の ⑴ ， ⑵ の中に，それぞれ７語以上の英語を補いなさい。（静岡県）

Ayaka： Hi, Nick. You look nice in that shirt.

Nick ： My mother got it for me on the Internet.

Ayaka： Buying clothes on the Internet is useful, because ⑴

Nick ： Last week, I visited a store near my house and got a shirt. Buying clothes in stores is sometimes better than on the Internet, because ⑵

Ayaka： I see.

16 次の⑴，⑵について，それぞれの指示に従って英語で書け。（愛媛県）

⑴ 次の①，②の質問に答える文を書け。ただし，①と②は，２つとも，それぞれ６語以上の１文で書くこと。（「,」「.」などの符号は語として数えない。）

① あなたは，夏休み中に，どのようなことをしましたか。

② また，そのとき，どのように思いましたか。

⑵ 海外の生徒たちと，オンラインで交流することになった。あなたが，自分たちの学校のよさを伝えるとしたら，どのように伝えるか。下の（　　）に当てはまるように文を書け。ただし，８語以上の１文で書くこと。（「,」「.」などの符号は語として数えない。）

Hello. Today, I'll tell you about our school.
(　　　　　　　　　　　　　　　　　　　　　　　　)
So we love our school.

17 次の条件に従って，あなたの意見を英語で述べなさい。（平安女学院高）

高校生になって，英語以外の言語を習う機会があるとしたら，あなたはどちらを選びますか。そして，それはなぜですか。

解答欄の［　　］内のどちらかを○で囲み，その理由を与えられた英語に続けて，15語以上の英語で述べなさい。与えられた英語は語数に含まず，また，英文は２文以上になってもよいこととします。

18 あなたは，英語の授業で，「スポーツをすることとスポーツをみることではどちらがよりおもしろいと思うか」というテーマで，英語で意見を伝え合うことになった。あなたならこのテーマについてどちらの立場で意見を述べるか。下の条件にしたがい，［ A ］，［ B ］にそれぞれ適当な英語を書き，あなたの意見を完成させなさい。（熊本県）

あなたの意見

I think ［ A ］ is more interesting because ［ B ］.

条件

・［ A ］には，選んだ方を2語以上の英語で書く。
・［ B ］には，その理由を4語以上の英語で書く。
・短縮形（I'm や isn't など）は1語と数え，コンマ（,）などの符号は語数に含めない。

15	(1)		
	(2)		
16	(1)	①	
		②	
	(2)		
17	I would like to choose [French : Korean], because		
18	A	I think　　　　is more interesting	
	B	because　　　　.	

3 英文法

例題1 ◀英文完成選択▶

□ (　　) に入る最も適切な語を，ア～エから１つ選び，記号で答えなさい。

(1) Ken and Yumi (　　　) each other for ten years. (京都明徳高)

ア　have known　　イ　has known　　ウ　knew　　エ　are knowing

アドバイス

「何の文法の問題なのか」を考える習慣をつけよう。

※例題：問題文にfor ten years（10年間）がある ⇒ 現在完了の問題と考えられる

文法ポイント：現在完了　動詞は〈have＋過去分詞〉になる。３つの用法の違いに注意！

(1) 完了　例：He has just finished his homework.（彼はちょうど宿題を終えた）
※よく使われる語句　just（ちょうど），already（すでに），yet（もう，まだ）

(2) 経験　例：I have been to Hawaii twice.（私はハワイに2回行ったことがある）
※よく使われる語句　once（1回），twice（2回），never（1度も～ない）

(3) 継続　例：I have known him for ten years.（私は彼を10年間ずっと知っている）
※よく使われる語句　for ～（～の間），since ～（～以来）

(2) They have (　　　) video games since this morning. (天理高)

ア　be played　　イ　be playing　　ウ　been played　　エ　been playing

差がつく文法：現在完了進行形

→動詞は〈have＋been＋～ing〉になる。

→用法は動作の継続（ずっと～している）だけ。

→文の動詞は「動作を表す動詞」が使われる。　※例：run（走る），walk（歩く）

They（彼らは） have been playing（ずっとしている） video games（テレビゲームを） since this morning.（今朝から）

【答】 (1) ア　(2) エ

例題2　◀同意文完成▶

□　次の2文がほぼ同じ内容になるように，（　　）に適切な語を入れなさい。

(1)　When I heard the news, I felt very happy.　（金光藤蔭高）

The news (　　　) (　　　) very happy.

アドバイス

2つの文の日本語訳の違いに注目しよう！

※例題　上の文：「私がその知らせを聞いたとき，とても幸せに感じました」

下の文：「その知らせは私をとても幸せにしました」

文法ポイント：第5文型　よく出るパターンを覚えておこう！

(1)　make A B　「AをBにする」

例：The news made me happy.（その知らせは私を幸せにした）

(2)　call A B　「AをBとよぶ」

例：We call her Mary.（私たちは彼女をメアリーとよんでいる）

(3)　keep A B　「AをBにしておく」

例：He always keeps his room clean.（彼はいつも部屋をきれいにしています）

(2)　I don't have much money now, so I can't buy that nice bag.　（報徳学園高）

If I (　　　) much money, I could (　　　) that nice bag.

差がつく文法：仮定法

→上の文：「私は今たくさんのお金を持っていないので，あのすてきなカバンを買うことができない」

下の文：「私がたくさんのお金を持っていれば，あのすてきなカバンを買うことができるのに」

※下の文は現実とは異なることなので，仮定法で表す。

→「もし～なら，…なのに」の文は〈If＋主語＋動詞の過去形，主語＋助動詞の過去形＋動詞の原形〉の語順になる。仮定法では，現在のことに対し，動詞や助動詞の過去形を使うことに特に注意しよう。

If I had much money, I could buy that nice bag.

（動詞の過去形：had　助動詞の過去形：could）

もし　私が　持っているなら　たくさんのお金を　私は　買うことができるのに　あのすてきなカバンを

had・could ―― 時制は現在!!

【答】 (1) made, me　(2) had, buy

§１．英文完成選択

1 次の文の（　　）に入る語句をア～ウから１つ選びなさい。　（京都西山高）

(1) There (ア is　イ are　ウ have) a lot of places to see in my town.

(2) (ア What　イ Why　ウ Which) do you like better, coffee or tea?

(3) My name is Yumiko. I am often (ア call　イ called　ウ calling) Yumi by my friends.

(4) We will not go on a hike (ア after　イ if　ウ although) it rains tomorrow.

(5) My brother has played soccer (ア for　イ since　ウ before) six years.

(6) I am the (ア tall　イ taller　ウ tallest) in my family.

(7) This cake is (ア her　イ their　ウ his).

(8) It's so hot today. (ア Will you　イ Shall I　ウ May I) open the window for me?

(9) She looked happy (ア hears　イ hearing　ウ to hear) the news.

(10) I don't know (ア what　イ where　ウ when) he lives. Tell me his address, please.

2 次の文が正しい文になるように，［　　］から適切なものを選び，記号で答えなさい。
（香ヶ丘リベルテ高）

(1) Hurry up, [ア and　イ or　ウ so] you will miss the train.

(2) Whose jacket is that? It's [ア me　イ my　ウ mine].

(3) I'm good [ア in　イ at　ウ on] making cakes.

(4) [ア Have　イ Did　ウ Do] you ever been to Hokkaido?

(5) February is the [ア two　イ twice　ウ second] month of the year.

3 次の各文の（　　）内で適切な語句を選び，記号で答えなさい。　（樟蔭東高）

(1) I'll show you the picture (ア who　イ which　ウ how) I took in Australia.

(2) Both Tom (ア or　イ and　ウ but) Ken are playing soccer now.

(3) People enjoyed (ア watch　イ to watch　ウ watching) the baseball game.

(4) Every child (ア have　イ has　ウ having) a different dream.

4 次の英文の意味が通るように，[　　　] に入る最も適切なものをア～エから選びなさい。

（大阪夕陽丘学園高）

(1) Andy [　　　] an apple yesterday.

ア eating　イ eaten　ウ ate　エ eats

(2) [　　　] use your pen? — Sure. Here you are.

ア Am I　イ May I　ウ Can you　エ Do you

(3) My dream is [　　　] a teacher.

ア became　イ become　ウ becomes　エ to become

(4) The boy [　　　] under the tree is my brother.

ア stand　イ stands　ウ standing　エ stood

(5) I must [　　　] my room now.

ア cleans　イ clean　ウ cleaned　エ cleaning

(6) Lucy is the [　　　] girl in her class.

ア most tall　イ taller　ウ tall　エ tallest

(7) [　　　] is really fun for me.

ア Sing　イ Singing　ウ Sang　エ Sings

(8) When [　　　] this huge temple built?

ア was　イ is　ウ did　エ do

(9) This is the bag [　　　] I bought last week.

ア which　イ who　ウ where　エ whose

(10) Kenta and Nick [　　　] playing tennis since I got here.

ア been　イ are　ウ have　エ have been

1	(1)		(2)		(3)		(4)		(5)		(6)	
	(7)		(8)		(9)		(10)					
2	(1)		(2)		(3)		(4)		(5)			
3	(1)		(2)		(3)		(4)					
4	(1)		(2)		(3)		(4)		(5)		(6)	
	(7)		(8)		(9)		(10)					

5 次の（　　）に入る最も適切なものをア～エからそれぞれ１つ選び，記号で答えよ。（東福岡高）

(1) I have (　　　) to do today.

ア a lot of homeworks　イ a lot of homework　ウ many homework
エ much homeworks

(2) When I visited my parents last night, they (　　　) dinner.

ア are having　イ have had　ウ have　エ were having

(3) Tom is really good at (　　　) soccer.

ア plays　イ to play　ウ playing　エ to be playing

(4) Have you ever (　　　) to Tokyo Skytree?

ア been　イ visited　ウ went　エ seen

(5) Mt. Fuji is higher than any (　　　) in Japan.

ア more mountain　イ more mountains　ウ other mountain　エ other mountains

6 次の(1)～(10)の英文について（　　）に当てはまる最も適切な語をア～エの中から１つずつ選びなさい。（昇陽高）

(1) He has (　　　) soccer for three years.

ア playing　イ been played　ウ been playing　エ being played

(2) If I (　　　) a bird, I could fly to you.

ア am　イ were　ウ be　エ been

(3) This medicine will (　　　) you sleep well.

ア make　イ do　ウ drink　エ take

(4) I wish I (　　　) his phone number.

ア were　イ am　ウ knew　エ knowing

(5) Tom finished (　　　) his room.

ア cleans　イ to clean　ウ cleaned　エ cleaning

(6) He and I (　　　) two dogs.

ア have　イ having　ウ to have　エ has

(7) Look at that boy (　　　) over there.

ア stand　イ to stand　ウ standing　エ stood

(8) John is ten years old. Ken is eleven years old. John is (　　　) than Ken.

ア older　イ oldest　ウ younger　エ youngest

(9) I have a friend (　　　) lives in Tokyo.

ア he　イ she　ウ who　エ which

(10) You (　　　) go to school today. Because it’s Sunday.

ア have to　イ don’t have to　ウ must　エ need to

§2．同意文完成

7 各組の英文がほぼ同じ意味になるように，(　　) に1語ずつ適語を入れなさい。 (大阪暁光高)

(1) Do you drive to work? — Do you go to work (　　　) (　　　)?

(2) I'm busy today, so I can't see you. — I (　　　) no (　　　) to see you today.

(3) He is our English teacher. — He (　　　) (　　　) English.

(4) Akira is not as old as Hiroshi. — Hiroshi is (　　　) (　　　) Akira.

(5) It began raining yesterday and it is still raining now. — It (　　　) (　　　) raining since yesterday.

8 各組の文がほぼ同じ内容を表すように，(　　) に適する語を書きなさい。 (梅花高)

(1) This computer is mine.
This is (　　　) computer.

(2) Shall we go shopping?
(　　　) go shopping.

(3) You must not speak Japanese in English class.
(　　　) speak Japanese in English class.

(4) There weren't any people in the park.
There were (　　　) people in the park.

(5) My town has three parks.
There (　　　) three parks (　　　) my town.

5	(1)		(2)		(3)		(4)		(5)			
6	(1)		(2)		(3)		(4)		(5)		(6)	
	(7)		(8)		(9)		(10)					

7	(1)			(2)			(3)		
	(4)			(5)					
8	(1)		(2)		(3)		(4)	
	(5)							

9 次の英文で，2つの文が同じ意味になるように空所に適切な語を入れなさい。　（プール学院高）

(1) Were you helped by the dog?
(　　) the dog (　　) you?

(2) Playing the violin is fun for me.
(　　) is fun for me (　　) play the violin.

(3) A year has twelve months.
(　　)(　　) twelve months in a year.

(4) Soccer is more popular than any other sport in England.
Soccer is the (　　) popular (　　) all the sports in England.

(5) She went to Paris last month and she is not here now.
She has (　　)(　　) Paris.

10 次の各組の英文がほぼ同じ意味になるように，(　　) にあてはまる語を1語ずつ書きなさい。

（大阪学芸高）

(1) I took a taxi to the museum.
I went to the museum (　　)(　　).

(2) I don't have enough time, so I can't visit the temple in the mountain.
If I (　　) enough time, I (　　) visit the temple in the mountain.

(3) Do you know the girl taking a picture over there?
Do you know the girl (　　)(　　) taking a picture over there?

(4) They do not understand the importance of keeping their hands clean.
They do not understand (　　)(　　) it is to keep their hands clean.

(5) Ken is the best swimmer in our class.
Ken (　　)(　　) than any other student in our class.

11 次の各組の英文がほぼ同じ意味になるように，(　　) 内に適切な語を1語ずつ入れなさい。

（神戸星城高）

(1) I can't finish this work without your help.
(　　) you (　　) help me, I can't finish this work.

(2) This city has many places to visit.
(　　)(　　) many places to visit in this city.

(3) I have a dog. It has blue eyes.
I have a dog (　　)(　　) blue eyes.

(4) They are all high school students.
All (　　)(　　) are high school students.

(5) I've never visited such a big city like Tokyo.
Tokyo is the (　　) city I've (　　) visited.

§3．正誤判断

12 次の各文の下線部には文法的に誤りのある箇所が１つあります。その記号を答えなさい。

（京都精華学園高）

(1) If we ア will leave now, we will イ arrive ウ there エ by noon.

(2) It looks ア like イ a banana, ウ don't エ it?

(3) How ア much イ are you ウ going to stay エ in China?

(4) She can ア swims イ as ウ fast エ as me.

(5) ア Do you know イ the language ウ using エ in Australia?

13 次の英文にはそれぞれ１箇所ずつ間違いがある。間違いの部分をア～エから選び，記号で答えなさい。

（清明学院高）

(1) I think he ア needs イ something ウ cold to エ drinking.

(2) ア Tom's father gave イ a watch him ウ when he passed the エ difficult exam.

(3) I ア know イ the boy ウ which エ painted this picture.

(4) ア We have イ many rain ウ in June エ in Japan.

(5) ア When イ is Ken ウ practicing soccer? — エ In the park.

9	(1)			(2)			(3)		
	(4)			(5)					
10	(1)			(2)			(3)		
	(4)			(5)					
11	(1)			(2)			(3)		
	(4)			(5)					

12	(1)		(2)		(3)		(4)		(5)	
13	(1)		(2)		(3)		(4)		(5)	

14 次の各英文について，文法的または語法的な誤りを含む下線部をア～エから１つずつ選び，記号で答えなさい。　　（開智高）

(1) I felt very（ア） sadly（イ） when I heard（ウ） the story about（エ） her.

(2) Is（ア） this book written（イ） by（ウ） Mr. Okada interested（エ） to you?

(3) This is the most（ア） beautiful flower that（イ） I have（ウ） never（エ） seen.

(4) While（ア） my stay（イ） in Yokohama, I saw（ウ） an old friend of mine（エ）.

15 次の(1)～(5)の英文の下線部には誤りの箇所がそれぞれ１つずつあります。その箇所をア～エの記号で選び，訂正して答えなさい。　　（金光八尾高）

(1) I ア live in Osaka, but イ I've ウ never エ gone to USJ.

(2) ア These pictures イ took ウ by my grandfather エ about 30 years ago.

(3) ア Could you stop イ to make so ウ much noise? エ I'm doing my homework.

(4) ア Do you イ know the woman ウ stand エ in front of the gate?

(5) My train arrives ア in 11:30. イ Can you ウ meet me エ at the station?

§４．語形変化

16 次の（　　）内の語を適切な形に直しなさい。形の変わらないものはそのまま書きなさい。なお，1語とは限りません。　　（金光大阪高）

(1) Ms. Kato (say) something to me when I left the classroom.

(2) Ken and I (be) in the library yesterday morning.

(3) This soup is (hot) than that.

(4) I know the (sing) girl very well.

(5) It stopped (rain) last night.

17 次の英文の（　　）内に入る最も適切な語を語群から１つ選んで記号で答え，正しい形に直しなさい。なお，それぞれの語は１度しか使えません。　　（関西学院高）

(1) Who was (　　) as the captain among the members of the basketball club?

(2) Brian is not at home right now. When he (　　) back, I'll tell him that you visited.

(3) The teacher showed me the book *Bocchan* (　　) by Soseki Natsume.

(4) I wish I (　　) enough money to buy a new smartphone.

(5) The train (　　) at 10:00 a.m. will take you there on time.

ア catch　　イ be　　ウ arrive　　エ write　　オ choose　　カ have

§5. 指示による文の書きかえ

18 次の英文を［　　］内の指示に従って書きかえなさい。　（大阪体育大学浪商高）

(1) You have to go to the post office.［疑問文に］

(2) Taro is older than Miki.［Mikiを主語にして，oldを用いて同意の文に］

(3) Mr. Smith has lived in Osaka <u>for ten years</u>.［下線部を尋ねる疑問文に］

(4) A day has 24 hours.［thereを用いて，同意の文に］

19 次の各文を（　　）内の指示に従って書きかえなさい。　（華頂女高）

(1) My brother drank <u>coffee</u> for breakfast.（下線部を問う文に）

(2) This is <u>her</u> book.（下線部を問う文に）

(3) A famous novelist wrote this book.（受動態の文に）

(4) Yukiko can play the violin.（過去形の文に）

14	(1)		(2)		(3)		(4)	

15		(1)	(2)	(3)	(4)	(5)
	記号					
	訂正					

16	(1)		(2)		(3)		(4)		(5)	

17		(1)	(2)	(3)	(4)	(5)
	記号					
	正しい形					

18	(1)	
	(2)	
	(3)	
	(4)	
19	(1)	
	(2)	
	(3)	
	(4)	

④ 会話文

ニューウイング出題率 63.2%

例題1 基本的なパターンを押さえよう

□ 次の対話が成立するように，①～⑤の（　　）内に入る最も適切なものを次のア～ケから選び，記号で答えなさい。 （四條畷学園高）

A： Hi, Kenta. Do you remember Yumi?

B： （　①　） We were in the same class in the first grade of junior high school. But she moved to Fukuoka. I haven't met her since then.

A： She will come to Tokyo with her family next month.

B： Really? （　②　）

A： She sent me an e-mail.

B： How long is she going to stay here in Tokyo?

A： （　③　）

B： I want to see her again. But I'm afraid that she won't remember me.

A： （　④　） Yumi and I often send e-mails to each other. When I asked Yumi about you, she said, "I remember Kenta well. He always talked about soccer with his friends."

B： Really? I'm so happy about that.

A： Also, she said she would bring us something good.

B： （　⑤　）

A： I don't know. But maybe it is something from Fukuoka.

B： I can't wait for next month.

ア Yes, I do.
イ No, I'm not.
ウ Why did she visit Tokyo?
エ For a week.
オ Please help yourself.
カ What is she going to bring?
キ Don't worry.
ク How did you know that?
ケ At two o'clock.

よく出る！　会話文挿入　前後のせりふに注目しよう！

① 直前のDo you remember Yumi?と直後のWe were in the same class in the first grade of junior high school.に注目。

→Aは「ユミを覚えている？」とたずね，B（ケンタ）は「僕たちは中学1年生のとき同じクラスだった」と答えた。このことから，Bはユミのことを覚えていたとわかる。

→ア「はい，覚えています」

② 直後のShe sent me an e-mail.に注目。

→Aは「彼女は私にメールを送ってくれた」と言っている。Bがたずねたのは，ユミが東京に来ることをAが知った方法である。

→ク「どうやってそれを知ったのですか？」

③ 直前のHow long is she going to stay here in Tokyo?に注目。

→Bは「彼女はここ東京にどのくらい滞在する予定なの？」とたずねているので，滞在する期間を答えるせりふが入る。

→エ「1週間です」

④ 直前のI'm afraid that she won't remember me.と2文後のWhen I asked Yumi about you, she said, "I remember Kenta well.に注目。

→「彼女は僕のことを覚えていないと思う」と言うBに対し，Aは「彼女は『ケンタのことをよく覚えている』と言っていた」と答え，Bのことを気づかっている。

→キ「心配しないで」

⑤ 直前のAlso, she said she would bring us something good.と直後のI don't know.に注目。

→Aは「彼女は私たちに何かよいものを持ってくると言っていた」と言い，それに対してBが何かを質問したあとに「わからない」と言っている。

→カ「彼女は何を持ってきますか？」

＋plus α よく出る会話表現

□ And you?	「あなたはどうですか？」
□ By the way, ～	「ところで，～」
□ Can you help me?	「手伝ってくれませんか？」
□ Certainly.	「たしかに」
□ Do you mean ～?	「あなたは～と言いたいのですか？」
□ Here you are.	「はい，どうぞ」
□ How about ～?	「～はいかがですか？」
□ How have you been?	「お元気でしたか？」
□ How was it?	「（それは）どうでしたか？」
□ I see.	「わかりました」
□ I'd like to ～.	「（私は）～をしたいのですが」
□ I'll take it(them).	「（買い物で）買います」
□ It sounds good.	「よさそうですね」
□ Let me see.	「ええと」
□ Long time no see.	「お久しぶりです」
□ May I help you?	「いらっしゃいませ」
□ Not yet.	「まだです」
□ Now I know that ～.	「～ということですね」
□ ～, right?	「～ですよね？」
□ That's too bad.	「お気の毒に」
□ You should ～.	「～すべきです」

【答】 ①ア　②ク　③エ　④キ　⑤カ

例題2　様々な問題形式に慣れよう

回　健司（Kenji）は，妹の美幸（Miyuki）と母親の由美（Yumi）に，学校で先生から与えられた宿題について話しています。会話文を読み，あとの問いに答えなさい。（金光八尾高）

Kenji　：Today my teacher told me something.

Yumi　：What was it?

Kenji　：She said to me, "Keeping a diary every day is important."

Miyuki：Keep a diary? Why?

Kenji　：I don't know. She said, "Think about why you should keep a diary. That is your homework." Do you know the reason, Mom?

Yumi　：Hey! Don't ask me, Kenji! That is your homework, isn't it?

Kenji　：Yes, but I have no idea. Have you ever kept a diary, Mom?

Yumi　：Yes, I have. I kept a diary when I was a high school student.

Kenji　：How was it?

Yumi　：At first, it was hard for me to write down daily things, [①] soon I *got used to it. By keeping a diary, I was able to *look back on the past and feel that I have grown up.

Kenji　：I see. Miyuki, you don't keep a diary, do you?

Miyuki：[　　②　　] I have never tried it. By the way, I hear that medalists in the Olympic Games keep a daily record about themselves.

Kenji　：My father told me that Otani Shohei, a professional baseball player, also kept a daily record and wrote down his ideas to improve his baseball skills in his school days. Now I know that successful people like him keep a daily record to *improve themselves. This must be the answer to the question that my teacher asked me!

Yumi　：Kenji, now you have finished your homework.

*get used to ～：～に慣れる　*look back on ～：～を振り返る　*improve：改善する

(1)　[①] に入れるのに最も適切なものを次から選び，記号で答えなさい。

ア　and　　イ　but　　ウ　finally　　エ　secondly

差がつく!!　語挿入（接続詞と副詞）　主語と動詞の数に注目！

At first, it was〈主語＋動詞〉 hard for me write down daily things, [①] soon I got〈主語＋動詞〉 used to it.

→空欄①を含む文には〈主語＋動詞〉が2つあるので，空欄には接続詞が必要。選択肢の中で接続詞はandとbut。（finallyとsecondlyは副詞）

→「最初，私にとって毎日のことを書きとめることは大変だった，[①] すぐに私はそれに慣れた」となるので，butが適切とわかる。

(2) [②] に入れるのに最も適切なものを次から選び，記号で答えなさい。

ア Yes, I do.　イ Yes, I don't.　ウ No, I do.　エ No, I don't.

差がつく!!　付加疑問文の答え方　Yesが「いいえ」，Noが「はい」になることに注意！

Miyuki, you don't keep a diary, do you?（美幸，日記はつけていませんよね？）

⇒ Yes, I do.（いいえ，つけています）　／　No, I don't.（はい，つけていません）

→否定文の付加疑問文に対する応答では，Yesが「いいえ」Noが「はい」の意味になることに注意しよう。

例1：You like soccer, don't you?（あなたはサッカーが好きですよね？）

⇒ Yes, I do.（はい，好きです）　／　No, I don't.（いいえ，好きではありません）

例2：You don't like soccer, do you?（あなたはサッカーが好きではないですよね？）

⇒ Yes, I do.（いいえ，好きです）　／　No, I don't.（はい，好きではありません）

(3) 会話文の内容として適切なものを次から２つ選び，記号で答えなさい。

ア Kenji's teacher told him to think about the importance of keeping a diary.

イ Kenji's mother did her son's homework instead of him.

ウ Kenji's sister keeps a daily record every day.

エ Kenji's mother kept a diary when she was a student.

オ Otani Shohei began to keep a daily record, but he was not able to improve his baseball skills.

よく出る!　本文内容一致　本文の該当箇所を探そう！

ア「健司の先生は彼に，日記をつけることの大切さについて考えるように言った」

→健司の2つ目と3つ目のせりふに「日記をつけることは大切です。なぜ日記をつけるべきかを考えてみましょう」という先生の発言がある。

イ「健司の母親は自分の息子の宿題を彼の代わりにした」

→母親（由美）の2つ目のせりふに Don't ask me. That is your homework, isn't it?（私に聞かないの。あなたの宿題よね？）とある。

ウ「健司の妹は日々の記録を毎日つけている」

→妹（美幸）の2つ目のせりふに「私は(日記を)つけていない。今までに試したことがない」とある。

エ「健司の母親は学生だったとき，日記をつけていた」

→母親（由美）の3つ目のせりふに「高校生のときに日記をつけていた」とある。

オ「大谷翔平は日々の記録をつけ始めたが，彼は野球の技術を改善することができなかった」

→健司の最後のせりふに「大谷翔平は日々の記録をつけ，野球の技術を改善した」とある。

【答】 (1) イ　(2) エ　(3) ア・エ

STEP UP

1 次の対話文を読み，各問いに答えなさい。（大阪産業大附高）

Clerk　：　①(いらっしゃいませ)
Woman：　Yes, please. ②【ア　buy / イ　like / ウ　a birthday present / エ　I'd / オ　to / カ　my father / キ　for】, but I can't decide what I should give him. Can you recommend something nice?
Clerk　：　Certainly. We have a lot of things in our shop. ③(　　)(　　) this tie?
Woman：　It's nice, but my father has ④(　　) retired. So I think he hardly ever uses ties.
Clerk　：　⑤(わかりました) Well, let me see... May I ask you some questions about your father?
Woman：　Yes.
Clerk　：　What is your father's ⑥(　　)?
Woman：　He ⑦(　　)(　　) a car.
Clerk　：　Then, how about these sunglasses? I think these are useful when your father is driving a car.
Woman：　They are very nice! ⑧(それを買います)
Clerk　：　Thank you very much.

【注】 recommend：～を薦める，推薦する　retire：退職する　hardly：ほとんど～しない
sunglasses：サングラス

⑴　下線部①，⑤，⑧の（　　）内の日本語に合うようにそれぞれ以下から英文を選び，記号を解答欄に書きなさい。
ア　I'll take them.　イ　Excuse me.　ウ　How much are they?　エ　I see.
オ　I'll call back later.　カ　May I help you?

⑵　下線部②が「私はお父さんの誕生日プレゼントを買いたい」という意味になるように【　　】内の語句を並べかえ，2番目と5番目になる語句の記号を書きなさい。

⑶　下記の日本語に合うように，下線部③，④，⑥，⑦の（　　）内に適切な語を1語ずつ入れなさい。
③　～はどうですか
④　すでに
⑥　趣味
⑦　運転するのが好きです

⑷　本文の内容に合うものを2つ選び，記号を解答欄に書きなさい。
ア　女性は弟の誕生日プレゼントを探していた。　イ　女性は何を買うか決めていた。
ウ　店員は最初にネクタイを薦めた。　エ　この店にはネクタイしかなかった。

オ　女性の父親はネクタイをよく使う。　　カ　女性はネクタイを買った。

キ　女性はサングラスを買った。

2 次の会話が自然な流れになるよう，文中の（ 1 ）～（ 5 ）に入れるのに最も適当なものを下のア～コの中から1つずつ選び，それぞれ記号で答えなさい。ただし，同じ記号は2度使えません。

（履正社高）

Bob：　Where will we have lunch?

May：　Well,（ 1 ）in front of the station.

Bob：　Oh, it is a nice idea, but I think（ 2 ）.

May：　Yes, probably it is. Then, do you have any idea?

Bob：　（ 3 ）?

May：　It sounds very good! I have never been there.

Bob：　（ 4 ）, but Mike said that it was very nice.

May：　He has eaten at a lot of restaurants, so（ 5 ）.

Bob：　OK, then hurry up. I'm hungry!

ア　I have never been there, either　　イ　it will not be a nice place　　ウ　I'm very hungry

エ　I want to try the new restaurant　　オ　it will be very nice

カ　it is crowded at this time　　キ　Shall I call that store

ク　What kind of restaurant is it　　ケ　How about that cafeteria

コ　Let's have lunch now

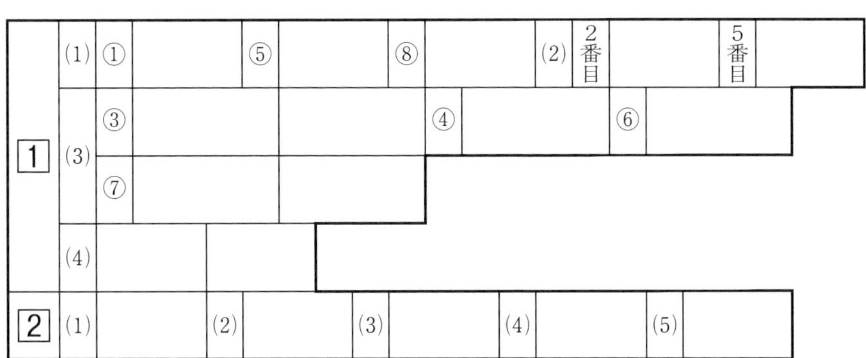
1 (1) ① ⑤ ⑧ (2) 2番目 5番目
(3) ③ ④ ⑥ ⑦
(4)
2 (1) (2) (3) (4) (5)

3 次の会話を読み，（ 1 ）～（ 6 ）に入る最も適切な英文を選択肢ア～キより１つずつ選び，記号で答えよ。ただし，同じ番号を２度以上使うことはできない。　（京都橘高）

(Kate and her host sister Yuki are talking in Kate's room.)

Yuki：Are you ready for our trip tomorrow, Kate?

Kate：Not yet. If you have finished packing, can you help me?

Yuki：Yes. Let me see... Oh, you want to take a lot of things.（ 1 ）It looks very heavy.

Kate：We are going to visit many famous temples, right? I can learn a lot about Japanese temples from that book. And... I need my camera.

Yuki：（ 2 ）You are good at taking pictures.

Kate：Thank you. I will take a lot of pictures during the trip.

Yuki：That's good.（ 3 ）

Kate：I think so, too. I'll give some of them to you and your family.

Yuki：Thanks, Kate. Well, you will not need your umbrella. I've checked the weather report.（ 4 ）

Kate：So I don't need my sweater, right?（ 5 ）

Yuki：But it will be very cold from tomorrow. You should take it.

Kate：OK. Oh, my bag is too small. Can I borrow your bag?

Yuki：Of course, but my mother has a better one.

Kate：Really?（ 6 ）Thanks, Yuki.

〈選択肢〉

ア　It will be fine during our trip.　イ　I'll ask her to lend it to me.

ウ　You should buy a new bag.　エ　Do you need to take this book?

オ　They will be good memories for us.　カ　Of course you should take that.

キ　It has been warm for a week.

4 次のアンダーソン夫人と娘のデビーとの対話を読んで，後の問いに答えなさい。　（清風高）

Debbie：Mom, I am home.

Mrs. Anderson：How was school? How did you do on the test?

Debbie：School was OK, and I did great on the test. Mom, I was so worried about that test, but now I feel great. ① What a relief!

Mrs. Anderson：I am glad to hear that. You have been studying so hard for the past few weeks. Now, you can relax and enjoy life.

Debbie：What are you cooking? [A]

Mrs. Anderson：I am baking cakes. This is your favorite banana cake.

Debbie：It looks really *yummy. I see *muffins over there, too. [B]

Mrs. Anderson：Yes. Jeff has to take something to school tomorrow. So, those muffins are for him. [C]

Debbie　　　　：Can I have a piece of banana cake? [D]

Mrs. Anderson：You don't want to wait until after dinner?

Debbie　　　　：It looks *inviting, and I'm sure it is delicious. No, I don't want to wait. Can I eat it now, Mom?

Mrs. Anderson：OK, ②go ahead.

Debbie　　　　：Did you see the new recipe that was posted on Today Cooking's website? I believe it was called Hawaiian Pie.

Mrs. Anderson：No, I didn't. But I want to try that recipe. Your dad loves pie.

Debbie　　　　：[E]

㊟ yummy：おいしい　muffin：マフィン　inviting：魅力的な

(1) 文中の [A] ～ [E] に入る適切なものを，次のア～オからそれぞれ1つずつ選び，記号で答えなさい。ただし，同じ記号を2回以上使ってはいけません。

ア Me, too.　イ It smells so good.　ウ Don't touch them.

エ I want to enjoy life right now.　オ You were busy, weren't you?

(2) 下線部①はDebbieのどのような気持ちを表しているのか，適切なものを次のア～エから1つ選び，記号で答えなさい。

ア 後悔　イ 安心　ウ 不安　エ 驚き

(3) 下線部②の内容として適切なものを，次のア～エから1つ選び，記号で答えなさい。

ア 食べていいですよ　イ 自分の部屋へ行きなさい　ウ こっちに来なさい

エ 一緒にしましょう

(4) 次のア～オの中で，本文の内容と合っているものを2つ選び，記号で答えなさい。

ア Debbie didn't study very hard, but she did well on the test.

イ Mrs. Anderson was making muffins for Debbie.

ウ When Debbie got home, her mother was making banana cake.

エ Debbie found muffins and she ate one of them.

オ Mrs. Anderson wants to try the new recipe posted on Today Cooking's website.

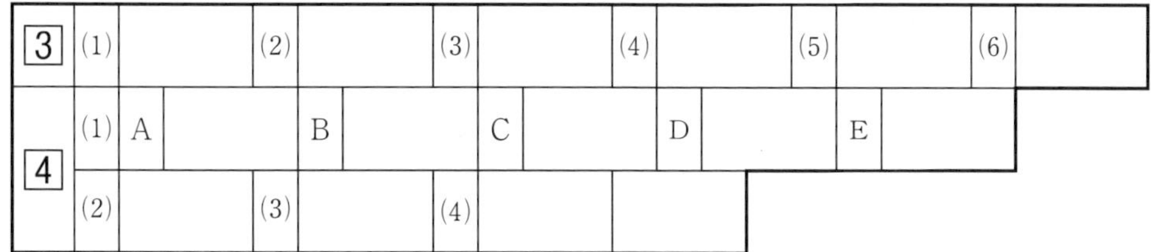

3	(1)		(2)		(3)		(4)		(5)		(6)	
4	(1) A		B		C		D		E			
	(2)		(3)		(4)							

5 次の対話文を読んで，後の問いに答えなさい。（園田学園高）

Sophie　：Hey, Matthew. ①Long time no see! How have you been?

Matthew：I've been great. [A] I heard that you went abroad during summer vacation.

Sophie　：I'm good, thanks. I went to Thailand and visited many famous places.

Matthew：I've never been to Thailand but I want to, someday. [B]

Sophie　：*Train Night Market in *Bangkok was my favorite. There are a lot of markets in Thailand and they are very popular with foreign visitors.

Matthew：You're right. But, why was Train Night Market your favorite? What's different from the other markets?

Sophie　：Markets are a fun place to enjoy buying some goods and eating local foods. But, Train Night Market is a little different because it has a beautiful night view.

Matthew：A beautiful night view? [C]

Sophie　：To see it, you need to go to a tall building. Then you can look down at the roofs of many *stalls at the market from there and the shape of the roofs looks *square. They also look like crowded square *jewels, when they are *illuminated by the light.

Matthew：Wow. That sounds interesting. If I go there someday, I will bring my camera and take some pictures of the view. By the way, did you join *Yee Peng Festival in Thailand during your stay? The festival is known to many people around the world as a *lantern festival. You can enjoy the wonderful view there, too.

Sophie　：My uncle who works for a tour company in Bangkok told me about it but I couldn't join it.

Matthew：Why not?

Sophie　：The festival is held every year between October and November but my trip was in August.

Matthew：[D] Next time, you should go. Anyway, there are so many interesting countries and places to visit in the world. Let's research them and make a list of places we would like to visit. Maybe, in the future, we can travel to all the places on the list together.

Sophie　：Yes. I can't wait for that.

（注）Train Night Market　トレインナイトマーケット　Bangkok　バンコク（タイの首都）
stall　屋台　square　四角の　jewel　宝石　illuminate　照らす
Yee Peng Festival　イーペン祭　lantern　ランタン

(1) 下線部①の日本語訳として最も適切なものを下のア～エから選び，その記号を答えなさい。

ア　はじめまして。　イ　ひさしぶり。　ウ　遅かったね。　エ　時間がないよ。

(2) 対話の流れに合うように [A] ～ [C] に入る最も適切なものを次のア～エから選び，その記号を答えなさい。

ア　What was the most wonderful place in Thailand for you?

イ　Did you take some pictures of the view?

ウ　I can't imagine it because it's a market.

エ　And you?

(3)　一般的なマーケット（市場）とトレインナイトマーケットの違いを本文の内容に沿って，日本語で簡潔に説明しなさい。

(4)　次の質問に対する答えが本文の内容に合うように，（　　）に入る語句を本文から抜き出し，答えなさい。

Question：Why do we need to go to a tall building?

Answer　：Because we can see and enjoy（　　）from there.

(5)　D　に「お気の毒に（残念だね）。」という意味の英文を書き入れなさい。

(6)　次のア～オの中から本文の内容に合うものを2つ選び，その記号を答えなさい。

ア　Matthew didn't know that Sophie went abroad during summer vacation.

イ　Many people around the world know Yee Peng Festival as a lantern festival.

ウ　Sophie enjoyed Yee Peng Festival during her stay.

エ　The purpose of Sophie's travel to Thailand was to meet her uncle who works for a tour company.

オ　Sophie and Matthew wish to travel to foreign countries together in the future.

5								
	(1)		(2) A		B		C	
	(3)							
	(4)	Because we can see and enjoy（　　）from there.						
	(5)					(6)		

6 次の英文は，静岡県でホームステイをしているジュディ（Judy）と，クラスメートの京子（Kyoko）との会話である。この英文を読んで，(1)〜(5)の問いに答えなさい。（静岡県）

（*After winter vacation, Judy and Kyoko are talking at school.*）

Judy　：Thank you for your New Year's card, *nengajo*. It was very beautiful, so I showed it to all of my host family.

Kyoko：[A] It is made of traditional Japanese paper called *washi*.

Judy　：I like *washi*, and my host family showed me an interesting video about it.

Kyoko：A video? [B]

Judy　：The video was about old paper documents in Shosoin. The paper documents were made of *washi* about 1,300 years ago. People have used *washi* since then.

Kyoko：That's very long! I didn't know that.

Judy　：When we read a variety（ ⓐ ）information written on *washi*, we can find things about the life in the past.

Kyoko：I see. *Washi* is important because we can（ ⓑ ）the long history of Japan, right? I've never thought of that. I'm happy I can understand Japanese culture more.

Judy　：By the way, where did you get the beautiful postcard?

Kyoko：I made it at a history museum.

Judy　：Do you mean you made *washi* by yourself?

Kyoko：[C] I made a small size of *washi*, and used it as a postcard.

Judy　：Wonderful! But making *washi* isn't easy.（ ⓒ ）I were you, I would buy postcards at shops.

Kyoko：Well... You love traditional Japanese things, so I wanted to make a special thing for you by using *washi*. It was fun to［ア　how　イ　think about　ウ　could　エ　create　オ　I］a great *nengajo*.

Judy　：Your *nengajo* was amazing! The *nengajo* gave me a chance to know an interesting part of Japanese culture. I found *washi* is not only beautiful but also important in your culture.

Kyoko：You taught me something new about *washi*, and I enjoyed talking about it with you. If you want, let's go to the museum. [　　　　]

Judy　：Yes, of course!

（注）card：あいさつ状　host family：ホストファミリー　be made of：〜から作られている
document：文書　Shosoin：正倉院（東大寺の宝庫）　past：過去
think of：〜について考える　by the way：ところで　postcard：はがき
by yourself：（あなたが）自分で　chance：機会

(1) 会話の流れが自然になるように，本文中の [A] 〜 [C] の中に補う英語として，それぞれア〜ウの中から最も適切なものを１つ選び，記号で答えなさい。

[A]　ア　I'm glad to hear that.　イ　Don't be angry.　ウ　I'll do my best.

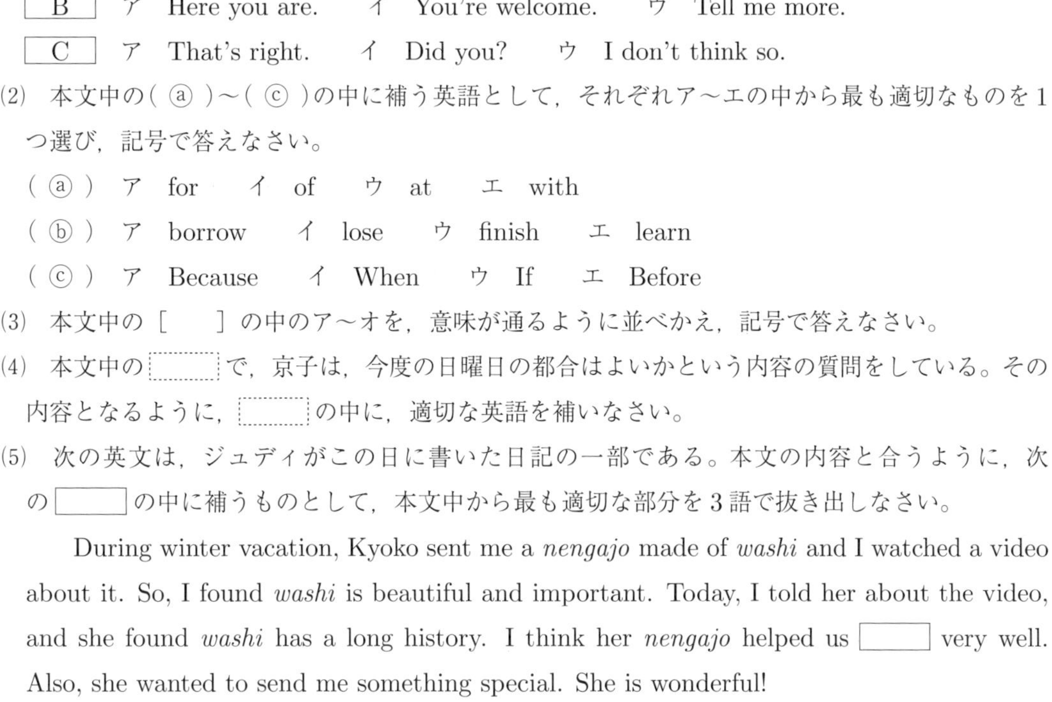

B　ア　Here you are.　イ　You’re welcome.　ウ　Tell me more.

C　ア　That’s right.　イ　Did you?　ウ　I don’t think so.

(2)　本文中の（ⓐ）～（ⓒ）の中に補う英語として，それぞれア～エの中から最も適切なものを1つ選び，記号で答えなさい。

（ⓐ）　ア　for　イ　of　ウ　at　エ　with

（ⓑ）　ア　borrow　イ　lose　ウ　finish　エ　learn

（ⓒ）　ア　Because　イ　When　ウ　If　エ　Before

(3)　本文中の［　　］の中のア～オを，意味が通るように並べかえ，記号で答えなさい。

(4)　本文中の［　　］で，京子は，今度の日曜日の都合はよいかという内容の質問をしている。その内容となるように，［　　］の中に，適切な英語を補いなさい。

(5)　次の英文は，ジュディがこの日に書いた日記の一部である。本文の内容と合うように，次の［　　］の中に補うものとして，本文中から最も適切な部分を3語で抜き出しなさい。

During winter vacation, Kyoko sent me a *nengajo* made of *washi* and I watched a video about it. So, I found *washi* is beautiful and important. Today, I told her about the video, and she found *washi* has a long history. I think her *nengajo* helped us ［　　］ very well. Also, she wanted to send me something special. She is wonderful!

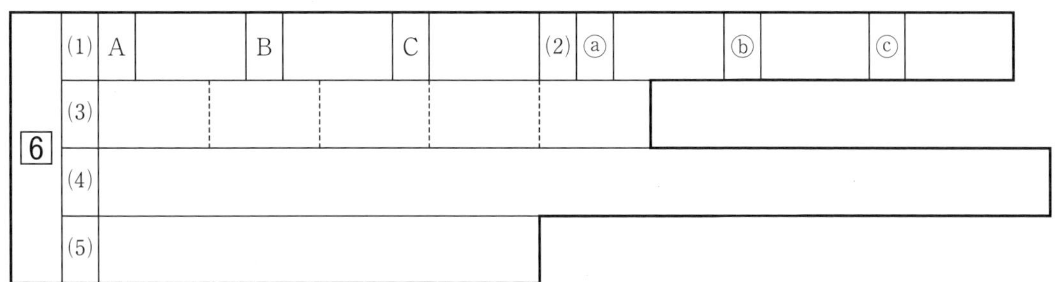

6												
	(1)	A		B		C		(2)	ⓐ		ⓑ		ⓒ	
	(3)											
	(4)											
	(5)											

Pick Up
そのほかのよく出る問題

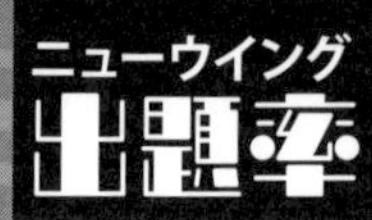

§1．問答・応答

1 次の各英文の質問に対する答えとして，最も適切なものを下記より選び，記号で答えなさい。ただし，同じ記号は一度しか使えません。 （大阪緑涼高）

(1) Do you come to school by bike?

(2) Whose textbook is this?

(3) Are you free tomorrow morning?

(4) May I help you?

(5) Would you please bring me some magazines?

(6) What time did you go to bed last night?

(7) Have you watched the movie yet?

(8) Shall we go to the movie next Saturday?

ア At eleven o'clock. イ It's Jasmine's. ウ Yes, I have. エ Sure. No problem.
オ No, I don't. カ Yes. I'm looking for a watch. キ Yes, let's. ク No, I'm not.

2 次の各対話の［　］内に入れるのに最も適切なものを１つ選び，記号で答えなさい。（育英高）

(1) A： How many countries have you ever visited in Europe?
B： ［　　］ I have visited France and two others.
ア One. イ Two. ウ Three. エ Four.

(2) A： Is this your computer, Mika?
B： ［　　］
ア Yes. It is yours. イ Go ahead, please. ウ I'll take it, please.
エ No. Mine is broken.

(3) A： Happy birthday, Takeshi. This is for you.
B： Thank you. ［　　］
ア You're kidding. イ May I open it? ウ Good for you.
エ I'm sorry to hear that.

(4) A： How about going out for lunch?
B： Sorry. ［　　］
ア That sounds good. イ How do you get there? ウ I'm meeting a friend.
エ Please make yourself.

3 次の(1)～(3)のそれぞれの問いかけに対する答えとして，適切な文を１つ選びなさい。（神戸第一高）

(1) Shall we go for a dinner tonight?

ア Yes, let's.　イ Yes, I am.　ウ No, we didn't.　エ No, I'm not.

(2) Have you ever met him?

ア Yes, I did.　イ Yes, I have.　ウ No, he didn't.　エ No, we have.

(3) Who do you think will win the game?

ア I'm trying now.　イ No, he won't.　ウ No, that's all.　エ He will.

4 次の(1)～(4)の会話文の［　　　］に入れるのに最も適しているものをそれぞれア～エから１つずつ選びなさい。（大阪府）

(1) A： What did you have for breakfast today?

B： ［　　　］

ア Yes, I did.　イ No, I didn't.　ウ I had it last night.　エ I had bread and milk.

(2) A： Can you help me?

B： ［　　　］

A： Thank you. Will you carry this box?

ア Yes, you will.　イ No, it isn't.　ウ It wasn't good.　エ Of course.

(3) A： Excuse me. Where is the station near here?

B： I'm sorry. ［　　　］ I am a visitor here.

A： That's OK, thank you. I will ask another person.

ア Yes, please.　イ No, thank you.　ウ I don't know.　エ You're welcome.

(4) A： I'm sorry. I'm late. Did we miss the train?

B： Yes, it's gone. Please don't be late again.

A： OK. ［　　　］ I'll come earlier next time.

B： I'm happy to hear that.

ア I won't be late.　イ I wasn't late.　ウ I don't understand.

エ I disagree with you.

1	(1)		(2)		(3)		(4)		(5)		(6)	
	(7)		(8)									
2	(1)		(2)		(3)		(4)					
3	(1)		(2)		(3)							
4	(1)		(2)		(3)		(4)					

5 次の(1)～(6)の対話文を読んで，(　　)に入る最も適当なものを，ア～エから１つずつ選び，記号で答えなさい。(甲子園学院高)

(1) A：(　　　　)
B：I want to send this letter to Tokyo. How much is it?
A：It's 94 yen.
ア Do you want some stamps?　イ Will you help me?　ウ May I help you?
エ Shall I send your letter?

(2) A：Hi. I went to the shopping mall yesterday.
B：(　　　　)
A：No, I didn't. I couldn't find anything to buy.
ア Did you buy anything?　イ Did you go there with your mother?
ウ How did you go there?　エ Were you with Emily?

(3) A：This is my favorite movie.
B：How many times have you watched the movie?
A：(　　　　)
ア Since I was four years old.　イ For three days.　ウ When I was in Tokyo.
エ Three times.

(4) A：I bought this bag yesterday.
B：It looks very nice. (　　　　)
A：It was 10,000 yen.
ア Can I borrow it?　イ How much did you have?　ウ How much was it?
エ You must like it!

(5) A：What are you going to eat?
B：I think I'll have curry and rice. (　　　　)
A：I'll have pasta.
ア Do you like pasta better than curry and rice?　イ Have you ordered something yet?
ウ How about you?　エ Which do you like, pasta or pizza?

(6) A：What are you going to do on Saturday?
B：Well, (　　　　)
A：I'm going to see a movie with Cathy. It is a very exciting action movie. Would you like to join us?
B：That sounds great!
ア I don't have any plans yet.　イ I want to see an action movie with you.
ウ I'm going to see a movie, too.　エ Sorry, but I will be busy on Saturday.

§2．絵や表を見て答える問題

6 次の広告を見て(1)，(2)の問いに答えなさい。 （神戸第一高）

Jin's cake shop

Opening hour: 8:30 a.m. to 7:00 p.m.

Closed: Wednesdays and during the New Year holidays

Try our new cheese cake!

(only 50 cents more)

a piece of banana cake with FREE coffee

Monday and Friday only

(1) What day of the week is this store closed?

ア Monday　イ Tuesday　ウ Friday　エ Wednesday

(2) What can the customer get for free?

ア cheese cake　イ banana cake　ウ sandwiches　エ coffee

7 次の英文を読み，円グラフの(1)～(4)に当てはまる料理をア～エの中から１つずつ選び，記号で答えなさい。 （滋賀短期大学附高）

We asked 100 people about their favorite dishes at ABC restaurant. This graph shows the *1rate. The most popular dish is chicken burger. We found that many young people like it. Beef steak is also one of the most popular dishes, but it is not as popular as curry and rice. The rate of spaghetti is half of beef steak. Pizza is especially popular with young men. Others are, for example, cheese burger, beef *2stew and sandwich.

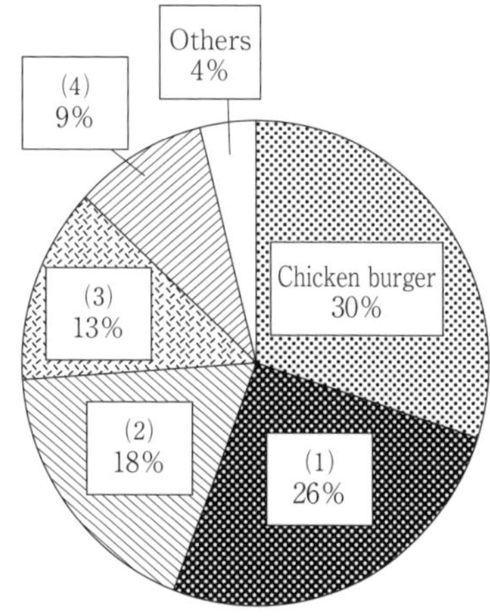

*1rate　割合　*2stew　シチュー

ア Spaghetti　イ Pizza　ウ Curry and rice

エ Beef steak

5	(1)		(2)		(3)		(4)		(5)		(6)	
6	(1)		(2)									
7	(1)		(2)		(3)		(4)					

8 Mika と Ken はバス停でバスを待っています。2 人の会話文を読み，Mika が乗るバスを下の時刻表の記号ア～エから選び記号で答えなさい。　（兵庫大附須磨ノ浦高）

Mika：　Excuse me.
Ken　：　Yes.
Mika：　It's already eight o'clock, but the bus hasn't come yet. Do you know why?
Ken　：　Which bus are you waiting for?
Mika：　This one.
Ken　：　Oh, it doesn't come because it's Sunday today.
Mika：　Then which one can I take?
Ken　：　Well, the earliest one is this.
Mika：　OK. I'll take it. Thank you.

Bus Schedule				
		6:30		▲6:50
ア▲7:05		7:30		▲7:50
イ▲8:05		ウ8:30		▲8:50
エ　9:05		9:30		9:50
10:05				
▲ No service on weekends				

9 次の番組表を見て，(1)～(3)の問いの答えとして正しいものを 1 つ選び，記号で答えなさい。　（常翔学園高）

Television Programs
Monday, February 10

	JBC Network（Channel 5）
6:00～8:00	*Morning Coffee* （news and entertainment）
8:00～8:30	*Eye on Style* （clothes from streets of Paris）
8:30～9:30	*More about Medicine* （latest health care）
9:30～10:00	*Travel Show* （today's travel：Singapore）
10:00～12:30	*Happy to Meet You* （morning movie：with Judy Green）
12:30～13:30	*Local News* （news and events today）

(1) How long is the movie?
　ア　One hour and thirty minutes　　イ　Two hours　　ウ　Two hours and thirty minutes

(2) When can you start watching a news program?
　ア　9:30　　イ　10:30　　ウ　12:30

(3) What is the 8:00 show about?
　ア　Travel　　イ　Fashion　　ウ　Coffee

10 次の対話文を読み，あとの設問に答えなさい。　　　　　　　　　　　　　　　（大阪産業大附高）

Mary： Excuse me. Can you tell me the way to the hospital?

Ken　： The hospital? Let me see. Go along this street. Then you'll see the（ ① ）on the third corner. Turn〔 ア 〕there and go straight. You'll find the hospital on your〔 イ 〕. It's between the post office and the（ ② ）. It's in（ ③ ）of the restaurant.

Mary： Thank you very much.

Ken　： No problem.

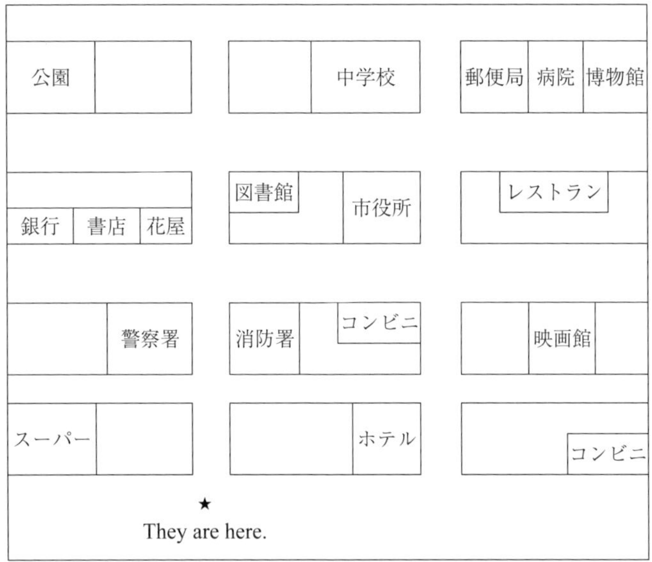

(1) 上の地図を参考に，対話文の（ ① ）～（ ③ ）に入る適切な英語を1語答えなさい。

(2) 対話文の〔 ア 〕〔 イ 〕内に入る適切な語を下から選び，答えなさい。

　ア　right / left

　イ　right / left

8												
9	(1)		(2)		(3)							
10	(1)	①		②		③		(2)	ア		イ	

11 右の絵を見て次の英文の（ 1 ）～（ 5 ）にあてはまる英語1語を答えなさい。　（日ノ本学園高）

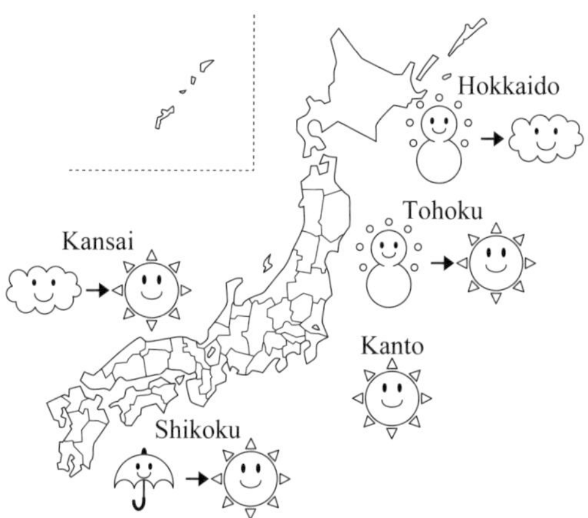

Now for the weather. Tomorrow morning we are going to have some rain in（ 1 ）and in some parts of Kyushu, but it's going to be sunny in the afternoon. The Kansai area（ 2 ）be a little cloudy in the morning, but afterwards it will be（ 3 ）. The Kanto area will be covered by a high pressure center and it will be sunny all day. Tohoku may have a little snow（ 4 ）the（ 5 ）, but it will be clear in the afternoon. In Hokkaido there will be snow in the morning and in the afternoon it will stop, but there probably won't be sunshine at all today.

12 次のグラフを見て(1), (2)の問いに答えなさい。　（神戸第一高）

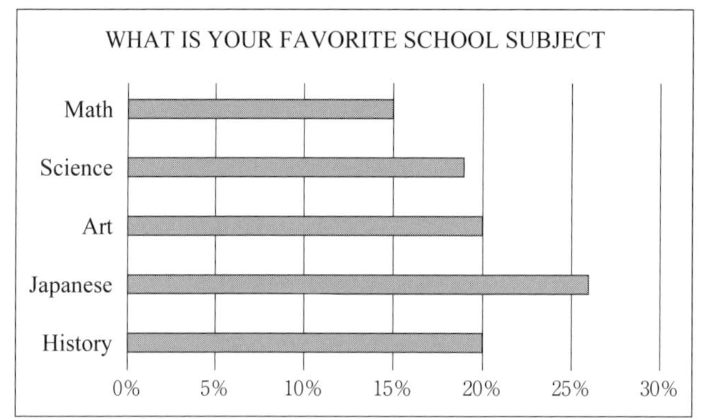

(1) How many students like math best?

ア 15%　イ 18%　ウ 20%　エ 26%

(2) What is the most popular subject?

ア Art　イ Japanese　ウ Science　エ Math

13 大学生のトムは “La Chicca” というオペラの座席を予約しようとしています。以下のウェブサイトの画面を参考に，あとの各文の（　　）内に入る最も適切な語(句)を選び，その記号を答えなさい。

（園田学園高）

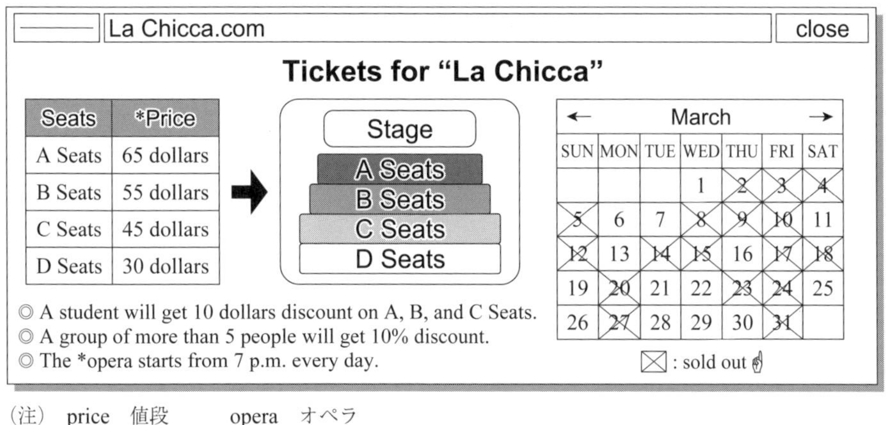

（注） price　値段　　opera　オペラ

(1) Tickets are sold out the most on (　　　) in March.

ア Mondays　イ Wednesdays　ウ Fridays　エ Sundays

(2) Tom's parents are free only on weekends, and Tom has a *Karate* lesson on Sunday evening. They can go to see the opera on (　　　).

ア March 4th or 11th　イ March 11th or 25th　ウ March 11th or 19th

エ March 19th or 26th

(3) Tom has to pay (　　　) if he buys C Seats tickets for himself and his parents.

ア 105 dollars　イ 115 dollars　ウ 125 dollars　エ 135 dollars

(4) Nancy is Tom's classmate. She is interested in the opera, so she wants to go to see it. If she goes with Tom and his parents, and they choose D Seats, they will get (　　　) discount.

ア 10 dollars　イ 20 dollars　ウ 10%　エ no

(5) They thought of buying two kinds of tickets; D Seats for Tom's parents and (　　　) for Tom and Nancy. In this case, they have to pay 150 dollars.

ア A Seats　イ B Seats　ウ C Seats　エ D Seats

11	(1)		(2)		(3)		(4)		(5)	
12	(1)		(2)							
13	(1)		(2)		(3)		(4)		(5)	

§3. 単　語

14 例にならって，各組のすべての単語に関連することばを，指定されたアルファベットで始まる英語1語で答えなさい。（芦屋学園高）

（例） koala / cat / panda [a _ _ _ _ _]　　答：a n i m a l

(1) eye / nose / mouth [f _ _ _]

(2) musician / doctor / engineer [j _ _]

(3) tomato / carrot / potato [v _ _ _ _ _ _ _ _]

(4) beef / chicken / pork [m _ _ _]

(5) hand / leg / head [b _ _ _]

15 次の(1)，(2)の文で説明しているものとして最も適当なものを，あとのア～エの中からそれぞれ1つずつ選び，記号を書きなさい。（佐賀県）

(1) This is something for writing or drawing. It is usually long.

ア desk　イ eraser　ウ pen　エ book

(2) Many students ride it to go to school. Many people use it when they have no time to walk.

ア bike　イ bed　ウ plane　エ chair

16 次の(1)，(2)の英文の□に入る最も適当な英語1語をそれぞれ語群から選んで書きなさい。

（北海道）

(1) We usually go to the □ to see many kinds of animals.

語群　station　factory　gym　zoo

(2) Blue, red, and green are the words for □.

語群　weeks　families　colors　numbers

17 次の（　）に，それぞれ与えられたアルファベットで始まる適切な語を1語入れ，英文を完成しなさい。（東海大付大阪仰星高）

(1) You can't travel abroad if you don't have a (p　　　).

(2) Do you know where my car keys are? I can't (r　　　) where I put them.

(3) September is the (n　　　) month of the year.

(4) After I (g　　　) from university, I want to work in a foreign company.

(5) I (w　　　) up late this morning and missed the bus.

18 次の英文の（　）内に入る語を答えなさい。ただし，指示された文字で始めること。（金蘭会高）

(1) Autumn is my favorite (s　　　) of the year.

(2) (M　　　) is the fifth month of the year.

(3) Our teacher told us to stay (h　　　) if we feel sick.

(4) (W　　　) comes after Tuesday.

19 次の(1)〜(5)のそれぞれの説明にあてはまり，右に示してある文字で始まる単語を答えなさい。ただし，答えは示してある文字も含めて解答欄に書きなさい。（上宮太子高）

(1) the second month of the year ［F　　］

(2) the day that comes after Friday ［S　　］

(3) a thing to use when we play tennis ［r　　］

(4) an animal which can fly in the sky ［b　　］

(5) a place which people visit to go abroad ［a　　］

20 次の各組のAの説明にあてはまる語をBの空所に入れ，Bを意味の通る英文にせよ。

（近大附和歌山高）

(1) A. a room that is used for cooking or washing dishes
B. Our mother is busy in the (　　).

(2) A. the eleventh month of the year, between October and December
B. The cold north winds begin to blow in (　　).

(3) A. a large area of water which is surrounded by land and it is larger than a pond
B. We went for a swim in the (　　).

(4) A. something that you use to protect yourself from the rain or hot sun
B. You should take an (　　) with you. It looks like rain.

(5) A. the warmest season of the year, between spring and fall
B. The (　　) vacation was very short last year.

(6) A. the part of the body at the end of the arm
B. It is important to wash your (　　)s before you eat.

(7) A. the brother of your mother or father
B. I'm going to visit my (　　) this weekend.

14	(1)	f	(2)	j	(3)	v	(4)	m	(5)	b
15	(1)		(2)							
16	(1)		(2)							
17	(1)	p	(2)	r	(3)	n	(4)	g	(5)	w
18	(1)	s	(2)	M	(3)	h	(4)	W		
19	(1)		(2)		(3)		(4)		(5)	
20	(1)		(2)		(3)		(4)		(5)	
	(6)		(7)							

21 次の英語の説明にあたる英単語を書きなさい。　（雲雀丘学園高）

(1) the ninth month of the year

(2) a person you have to see when you are sick

(3) a place you go to when you want to borrow some books

(4) a book you can use if you want to know the meaning of a word

22 次の各文の（　　）には，発音は同じでつづりの違う語が入ります。意味が通じるように，（ ア ）と（ イ ）に入る適切な語をそれぞれ書きなさい。　（東大谷高）

(1) He was very angry and (ア) his pen at the wall.
She went (イ) the room to the kitchen.

(2) Can you say your name again? I didn't (ア) you.
He came (イ) two days ago.

(3) We are going to (ア) in front of the station next Friday.
I ate (イ) for dinner last night.

(4) I wash my (ア) every day.
Would you (イ) the door when you go out?

(5) I (ア) a bus to school when I was a high school student.
There are a lot of cars on the (イ).

§4．相関単語表

23 次のＣとＤが，ＡとＢの関係になるようにＤの（ 1 ）～（ 5 ）に入る適切な単語を答えなさい。
（大阪暁光高）

A	B	C	D
one	first	three	(1)
dance	dancing	run	(2)
box	boxes	child	(3)
write	written	break	(4)
tall	tallest	good	(5)

24 A欄とB欄の関係と，C欄とD欄の関係が同じになるように，（ 1 ）～（ 5 ）に最も適切な単語を書きなさい。（大阪薫英女高）

A	B	C	D
sun	day	moon	（ 1 ）
doctor	hospital	teacher	（ 2 ）
I	mine	they	（ 3 ）
in	out	up	（ 4 ）
take	took	put	（ 5 ）

25 次の(1)～(5)において，それぞれのCとDの関係がAとBの関係と同じになるように，Dにあてはまる最も適当な1語を，英語で答えなさい。（甲子園学院高）

	A	B	C	D
(1)	speak	spoken	throw	
(2)	come	came	leave	
(3)	book	books	knife	
(4)	north	south	east	
(5)	father	mother	son	

21	(1)		(2)		(3)		(4)	

22		(1)	(2)	(3)	(4)	(5)
	ア					
	イ					

23	(1)		(2)		(3)		(4)		(5)	
24	(1)		(2)		(3)		(4)		(5)	
25	(1)		(2)		(3)		(4)		(5)	

26 次のCとDの関係がAとBの関係と同じになるように，それぞれの（　　）に適切な語を入れなさい。　　（大阪電気通信大高）

	A	B	C	D
(1)	play	played	cry	(　　)
(2)	5	May	11	(　　)
(3)	drink	drunk	do	(　　)
(4)	we	ours	I	(　　)
(5)	small	smallest	well	(　　)

27 次の各組のCとDの関係がAとBの関係と同じになるように，（　　）に入る適語を答えなさい。　　（好文学園女高）

	A	B	C	D
(1)	short	long	heavy	(　　)
(2)	book	books	story	(　　)
(3)	see	seen	draw	(　　)
(4)	my	myself	their	(　　)
(5)	won	one	piece	(　　)

28 次の各語について，CとDの関係がAとBの関係と同じになるように，（　　）内に適切な語を入れなさい。　　（京都精華学園高）

	A	B		C	D
(1)	you	your	:	it	(　　)
(2)	is not	isn't	:	will not	(　　)
(3)	first	January	:	seventh	(　　)
(4)	tall	tallest	:	bad	(　　)
(5)	hot	cold	:	same	(　　)

26	(1)		(2)		(3)		(4)		(5)	
27	(1)		(2)		(3)		(4)		(5)	
28	(1)		(2)		(3)		(4)		(5)	

解答・解説 英語

1．長文問題（P. 12～25）

〈解答〉

1 (1)(i) イ　(ii) ア　(iii) エ　(iv) ウ　(v) イ　(2)(A) イ　(B) エ　(C) ア　(D) ウ　(E) ア　(3) ① ×　② ○　③ ×　④ ×　⑤ ○　(4) エ　(5) 猫を家に連れて帰りたかったから。（同意可）　(6) I couldn't leave him there　(7) 私はその猫をトビーと名付けるわ。

2 (1) ① ウ　⑦ イ　(2) ② told　③ shocked　⑤ drew　(3) ④ 私たちの未来を壊さないで。⑧ あなたの声は世界を変える力を持っている。(4) she wanted people to know　(5) ① ○　② ○　③ ○　④ ×　⑤ ×　(6) ア・エ　(7) ① adults, global, warming　② Fridays, for, Future

3 (1) エ　(2) like, to, you　(3) 絵画を理解することは難しい。(4) ㊤ イ　㋙ ウ　(5) ㋔ エ　㋕ ア　㋗ ウ　(6) ア　(7) イ　(8) イ　(9) ア　(10) イ　(11) イ・エ

4 (1) ① ア　② エ　③ ウ　④ イ　⑤ エ　(2) イ　(3) ウ　(4) 見つけにくい（同意可）　(5) ウ・オ・キ

5 (1) ① ア　② ウ　③ ウ　(2)（例） They were in Yuki's house　(3) イ　(4) A. ゆっくり歩く　B. 話を聞く　C. 手伝いすぎる（それぞれ同意可）　(5) ウ

6 (1) あ. ア　い. ウ　う. エ　(2) 1. イ　2. エ　3. ウ　(3) エ　(4) ② 海の中の魚がマイクロプラスティックを食べ続けていること。⑥ プラスティック汚染を止めること。（それぞれ同意可）　(5) The environmental problems with plastic　(6) プラスティック汚染を止めるために私たちは何かをしなければならない。(7) There are two things we can do right　(8) ア・カ

7 (1) social, media　(2) A　(3)（ソーシャルメディアを使うことは）若い人々に悪い影響を与える（ということを）いくつかの研究が示した（。）（同意可）　(4) イ　(5) spend time with friends on social media　(6)（4番目）ウ　（6番目）オ　(7) ア　(8) イ・オ

1 (1)(i) トビーは「木の下で子猫を『見かけた』」。過去の出来事を語っているので，文の前半と同じく過去形が入る。(ii) be lost ＝「迷子になる」。(iii) just then（ちょうどそのとき）は過去を表す表現なので，過去形を選ぶ。(iv)「女の子は子猫のところに『走った』」。過去形が適切。(v)「トビーはずっと気分よく『感じた』」。過去形が適切。(2)(A) トビーが木の下で見つけたのは「子猫」。(B) 保護施設に連れていったら「いい家を与えてもらえる」のは，トビーが2日続けて連れ帰った2匹の「子猫」。(C) 女の子の母親が，子猫を見つけた「トビー」に対して言った言葉。(D)「もう出ていってほしくない」のは，壁の穴を抜け出してしまった2匹の「子猫」のこと。(E) 女の子と彼女の母親は，「トビーと彼の母親」が子猫にしてあげた care（世話）に対して感謝した。(3) ① 第1段落の2文目を見る。トビーは犬と猫を飼っているが，鳥は飼っていない。② 第2段落を見る。on one's way to the movies ＝「映画に行く途中で」。正しい。③ 第3段落の最終文を見る。子猫に餌をあげたのはトビーではなく，彼の母親である。④ 第6段落の中ごろを見る。子猫は捨てられたのではなく，壁の穴を抜けて外へ出てしまった。⑤ 最終段落の後半を見る。女の子の母親はトビーを「いつでも歓迎する」と言っている。正しい。(4) enough ＝「十分な」。so ＝「だから」。not ～ any more ＝「もうこれ以上～ない」。(5) 直後に書かれている，「トビーが映画を諦めてしたこと」に着目する。(6)「A をそこに放っておく」＝ leave A there。(7) be going to ～＝「～するつもりである」。name A B ＝「A を B と名付ける」。

【全訳】 トビーは動物が大好きでした。彼は家で2匹の犬と1匹の猫を飼っており，そして鳥も手に入れたい

と思っていました。彼のお母さんは，彼には十分な数のペットがいるので，それ以上は飼えないと彼に言いました。

ある日トビーは，映画を観に行く途中で，木の下に子猫を見かけました。

「どうしたの？」とトビーは子猫にたずねました。「誰かが君を家に連れて帰るのを忘れたの？」 子猫はとても幼く見え，ひどく怖がっているようでした。トビーは映画を諦め，子猫を自分の家に連れて帰ることに決めました。「トビー，そこに何を持っているの？」とお母さんがたずねました。「柳通りの木の下で彼を見つけたんだ」とトビーは言いました。「彼には名札がついていないから，僕は彼を家に連れ帰るべきだと思ったんだよ」「あなたにはもう十分な数のペットがいるわ，トビー」「でもお母さん，僕はそこに彼を放ってはおけなかったよ」 お母さんはその子猫に牛乳と食べものをあげました。

その翌日，トビーが学校から帰っていると，また別の子猫を見つけました！ 「おや，君も迷子なの？」 トビーはその子猫も家に連れて帰りました。「トビー，あなたはこの２匹の子猫たちを飼うことはできないわ！」とお母さんが言いました。「私たちは彼らを保護施設へ連れていきましょう，そうすれば他の誰かが彼らにいい家を与えてくれるわ」 トビーは子猫たちを飼えないことを悲しく思いました。

トビーとお母さんはその翌日，保護施設へ子猫たちを連れていきました。保護施設の役人は彼らを歓迎しました。

ちょうどそのとき，小さな女の子とお母さんが保護施設の中に入ってきて，子猫たちを見つけました。「ママ，見て，子猫たちがあそこにいるわ！」 小さな女の子は子猫たちのところへ走っていきました。「あの子たちは私の子猫よ！」と女の子は叫びました。彼女のお母さんは，彼らはおそらく壁の小さな穴から抜け出したのだろうと言いました。トビーはその女の子に言いました，「僕は柳通りで彼らを見つけて，面倒を見るために家に連れて帰ったんだ」

「あなたが彼らを見つけてくれて，私たちはとても嬉しいわ」と女の子のお母さんは言いました。トビーは，子猫たちが安全で，いい家庭にいられるのだとわかり，気持ちがずっと楽になりました。「私たちは壁を修理しなければならないわね」と女の子のお母さんは言いました。「もう彼らには出ていってほしくないから」

彼女たちは２人はとも，トビーと彼のお母さんが子猫を世話してくれたことに感謝しました。女の子は猫の１匹を抱き上げました。「私はこの子をトビーと名付けるわ」と女の子は言いました。トビーはにっこり笑い，自分は子猫たちに会いに行くつもりだと言いました。「いつでも歓迎するわ」と女の子のお母さんは言いました。トビーは子猫たちに笑いかけ，さよならを言いました。

2 (1) ① be born in ～＝「～で生まれる」。⑦ グレタが自己紹介をしている。from ～＝「～出身で」。(2) ② was told to ～＝「～するよう言われた」。③ was shocked to ～＝「～してショックを受けた」。⑤ draw attention −「注目を引く，集める」。過去形にする。(3) ④ Do not ～＝「～しないで」。destroy ～＝「～を壊す」。⑧ 不定詞の形容詞的用法で，to 以下が the power を後ろから修飾する。the power to ～＝「～する力」。(4) wanted A to ～＝「A に～してほしい」。(5) ① 第１段落の６文目参照。正しい。② 第１段落の６文目参照。正しい。③ 第１段落の 10 文目参照。正しい。④ 第２段落の８文目参照。前文に 2018 年のできごとが書かれており，その１年後なので，グレタは 2019 年に国連でスピーチをした。⑤ 第２段落の４文目参照。グレタは小さくても変化を起こすことができると思っている。(6) ア.「ルールに従うことでは世界を救えない」。第２段落６文目参照。合っている。イ.「気候のための学校ストライキが問題を解決するための唯一の方法だ」とは言っていない。ウ. 第２段落７文目参照。「すべてのことが変えられるべきだ」とは言っているが，「学校」に限定して言っているのではない。エ.「世界の指導者はいつもお金のことを話している」。第２段落最後から３文目参照。合っている。(7) ①「グレタはなぜ腹を立てたのですか？」。第１段落の中ほどを見る。「『大人』が『地球温暖化』を止めるために何もしなかったから」。②「グレタの運動は何と呼ばれていますか？」。第１段落の最後の文を見る。「それは『未来のための金曜日』と呼ばれている」。

【全訳】 グレタ・トゥンベリは 2003 年にスウェーデンで生まれました。彼女は８歳のとき，初めて気候変動について聞きました。彼女はエネルギーを節約するために電気を消し，紙をリサイクルするよう言われました。学校で，彼女は海のゴミの映画を見て，ショックを受けました。彼女は地球温暖化を止めるために何もしなかった大人に腹を立てました。彼女が15歳のとき，学校に行かずに毎日一人で国会の前の地面に座ることを決めました。彼女は「気候のための学校ストライキ。私たちの未来を壊さないで」と書かれた看板を持っていました。彼女の声はすぐに注目を集めました。多くの若者が金曜日に世界中で座り，ストライキを始めました。この大きな運動は「未来のための金曜日」と今では呼ばれています。

グレタは，私たちの世界には問題があるということを人々に知ってほしかったので，声をあげました。「私の名前はグレタ・トゥンベリです。私は15歳で，スウェーデン出身です。多くの人々がスウェーデンはとても小さな国だと言いますが，小さすぎて変化を起こすことができないものはないと私は学びました。学校ストライキを始めたとき，私は学校に行って勉強すべきだという人がいました。しかし，私たちはルールに従って行動することで世界を救うことはできません。すべてのことが変えられるべきです」と彼女は2018年に言いました。1年後に国連で，彼女はスピーチをしました。「私は学校に戻るべきです。あなたたちが私の夢を奪ったのです。しかし私は幸運な人間の一人です。人々は苦しんでいます。人々は亡くなっています。生態系全体が崩壊しています。私たちは大量絶滅の始まりにいます。ところが，あなたたちはいつもお金のことばかり話します。よくもそんなことを！」 グレタは2019年にノーベル平和賞にノミネートされました。

何か間違ったことがあれば，あなたは声をあげることができます。あなたはインターネットを使ったり，友達や家族と話したり，あるいは国会に手紙を書いたりすることができます。あなたの声は世界を変える力を持っています。あなたの未来はあなたの手の中にあります。

3 (1) サチコは聞き手に「あなた方は絵画を見ることが好きですか？」と問いかけているので，スピーチの話題は「美術」だとわかる。(2)「〜したい」= would like to 〜。I'd は I would の短縮形。「A に 1 つ質問をする」= ask A a question。(3) them は前述の複数形の名詞 paintings を指している。it is 〜 to …=「…することは〜である」。(4) ㊁ the other day があることから，過去の文とわかる。give の過去形は gave。㋙ 主語 The paintings（＝もの）が to you（＝人にとって）「興味深い」場合は，interesting を用いる。(5) ㋔ 前文に「象徴の意味を学ぶことによって，簡単に有名な人物を見つけることができます」とあり，その例としてマリアの説明を続けているので，「例えば」の意味の For example が適切。㋕ マリアの象徴に続けて，アポロ神の象徴について説明しているので，「さらに」の意味の Also が適切。㋗「この形（＝三角形）を見ると，安心とくつろぎを感じるでしょう」と「三角形の構図は平和的な絵画で使われます」をつなぐので，「この理由で」という意味の For this reason が適切。(6)「象徴のルールを学んでください，そうすれば，絵画の中で大好きな人物を見ることがおもしろくなるでしょう」。「〜しなさい，そうすれば…」=〈〜(命令文), and …〉。(7)「どんな理由でも大丈夫なので，自由に考えてください」。「どんな〜でも」= any 〜。(8) 三角形の構図について，「この形を見ると，安心とくつろぎを感じるでしょう」と説明されている。(9) 三角形の構図について，「主要な人物たちは絵画の真ん中にいて，三角形を形づくります」と説明されている。(10) アポロ神について，「アポロは通常，音楽を演奏して，葉で作られた王冠をかぶっています」と説明されている。(11) ア．第2段落の1文目を見る。花や動物の生態を知るのではなく，絵画の中に花や動物のような象徴を見つけるようにする必要がある。イ．第2段落の前半を見る。「象徴の意味を学ぶことによって，簡単に有名な人物を見つけることができます」とあるので正しい。ウ．第3段落の1文目を見る。「もし構図について知るなら，絵画をより楽しむことでしょう」とある。エ．第4段落を見る。絵画を見るのに最も重要なのは，好きな絵画を「なぜ好きなのか？」と自分自身に問いかけ，その理由を他人に話すことだとあるので正しい。オ．「好きな絵画だけを見ること」がコツだという内容はない。

【全訳】 こんにちは，みなさん。私はサチコです。私は今日の話題として「美術」を選びました。私のスピーチを始める前に，私はあなた方に1つ質問がしたいです。あなた方は絵画を見るのが好きですか？ あなた方はそれらを理解することは難しいと考えるかもしれません。実際，私もまた，初めて美術館を訪れたとき，そのように思いました。しかしながら，先日，私の美術の先生が，私にそれを楽しむための3つのヒントを与えてくれました。あなた方にそれらを紹介させてください。

まず，絵画の中に花や動物，あるいは衣服のようないくつかの象徴を見つけるようにしてください。それらを見つけたら，それらの背後にある意味を考えるようにしてください。象徴の意味を学ぶことによって，簡単に有名な人物を見つけることができます。例えば，青色はイエス・キリストの母親であるマリアの象徴なので，彼女はよく青色の服を着ています。もしこのルールを知っているなら，絵画で彼女を見つけることは簡単でしょう。さらに，ギリシア・ローマ神話の絵画では，太陽の神であるアポロは通常，音楽を演奏して，葉で作られた王冠をかぶっています。象徴のルールを学んでください，そうすれば，絵画の中で大好きな人物を見ることがおもしろくなるでしょう。

次に，もし構図について知るなら，絵画をより楽しむことでしょう。三角形の構図は最も一般的です。この構図においては，主要な人物たちは絵画の真ん中にいて，三角形を形づくります。この形を見ると，安心とくつろぎを感じるでしょう。この理由で，三角形の構図は平和的な絵画で使われます。

最後に，最も重要なのは，絵画を見るとき，感情に正直になってください。好きな絵画を見るとき，自分自身に「なぜ私はこれが好きなのだろうか？」と問い，その理由を他人に話してください。どんな理由でも大丈夫なので，自由に考えてください。次には，自分のお気に入りの絵画をよりたやすく見つけることができます。

絵画の中に何を探すべきかを知るなら，絵画を見ることをより楽しむことでしょう。美術館を訪れるとき，上記の点について考えてください。絵画はあなた方にとってより興味深く見えるかもしれません。

4 ⑴ ① probablyの前にwillがあるので原形になる。② 過去の文で，あとに複数形の名詞が続くのでwereになる。③ There haveで始まっているので現在完了〈have＋過去分詞〉の文である。④ 現在の文であとに単数形の名詞が続くのでisになる。⑤「この理由のため，私たちはとても注意深くなり，フロリダのマナティーの数をチェックし続けなければならない」という意味になる。「～しなければならない」＝ have to ～。have toのあとの動詞は原形になる。⑵ 直前の2文を見る。大部分の哺乳動物は首に7つの骨があるが，マナティーは6つしか持っていない。これがマナティーが振り向くことができない理由である。⑶「多くの人々はすぐにすべてのマナティーが亡くなってしまうだろうと心配していた」という意味になる。「～ということを心配している」＝ be worried that ～。⑷ 直前に「これらの人々が使うボートはとても速く進むので，水面の近くで泳いでいる灰色のマナティーを見つけることが困難である」と書かれており，これがマナティーのボート事故の原因だと考えられる。⑸ ア．第1段落の中ごろを見る。マナティーは1頭で泳ぐことが多く，グループで泳ぐ時も少数である。イ．第1段落の最終文を見る。マナティーは短い時間しか速く泳ぐことはできない。ウ．「1970年代以降，マナティーの数は増えた」。第4段落の4文目を見る。1970年代以降のフロリダのマナティーについて，「その時以来，その数は増えていき，今は6,000頭以上いる」と書かれているので，内容にあてはまる。エ．マナティーがしばしば魚を食べるとは書かれていない。オ．「水の汚染がマナティーの死の1つの原因である」。第5段落を見る。川の汚れが原因で川底の草が育たず，マナティーの食べ物が不足して亡くなると書かれているので，内容にあてはまる。カ．第6段落の1文目を見る。マナティーは夏になり水が温かくなると，海へ移動する。キ．「フロリダの人々がマナティーの数を増やすことはとても困難である」。最終段落の2文目を見る。内容にあてはまる。

【全訳】 マナティー

マナティーは世界の数か所にしか住まない，大きくゆったりとした，平和的な動物です。彼らは40年間生きることができ，600キログラムまで成長します。3種類のマナティーがいて，彼らはアメリカ合衆国，南米，そしてアフリカの地域に住んでいます。マナティーは静かな生活を送ります。彼らはよく1頭だけで泳ぎます。もしあなたが一緒にいるマナティーのグループを見かけたら，それはおそらく6頭以下の小さなグループでしょう。彼らは通常，時速約8キロメートルで，ゆっくりと泳ぎます。彼らは時速24キロメートルのスピードまで到達することができますが，ほんのわずかな時間だけしかその速度で泳ぐことができません。

マナティーは哺乳動物です。赤ん坊が幼い時，彼らは彼らの母親からミルクを飲みます。しかし，彼らは興味深い点で，他の哺乳動物とは異なっています。犬，ネコ，人間，そしてキリンを含む，大部分の哺乳動物は首に7つの骨があります。マナティーは6つしか持っていません。このことは，彼らが自分たちの後ろを見るために，振り向くことができないことを意味します。彼らはゆっくりと体全体を回さなければなりません。マナティーの目は小さいですが，彼らはとてもよく見ることができます。しかしながら，彼らの異なる首のせいで，彼らは自分たちの前にあるものしか見ることができません。

マナティーを見るための最もよい場所の1つは，アメリカ合衆国の中で美しい自然を持つ場所であるフロリダにあります。

1970年代，フロリダにはほんの数百頭のマナティーしかいませんでした。多くの人々はすぐにすべてのマナティーが亡くなってしまうだろうと心配していました。彼らはマナティーの川をきれいにするために一生懸命働き，夏にボートから彼らを守るための法律を作りました。その時以来，その数は増えていき，今は6,000頭以上います。しかしながら， 2021年の今，マナティーは再び危機にあります。この年の前半には，2020年の1年間全てよりも多くのマナティーが亡くなりました。

今年，より多くのマナティーが亡くなりつつある理由は，彼らが食べるための十分な食べ物がないということです。健康なマナティーは毎日その体重の約10％を食べなければなりません。冬に，マナティーはフロリダの川の底で育つ草を食べます。最近，フロリダにより多くの人たちが住んでいるので，これらの場所の水は汚染により汚れてしまっています。太陽からの光が川の底に到達することができないので，草が育つのは困難になっています。

夏には，水がより温かくなるので，マナティーは海へ移動します。そこで，彼らはより多くの場所とより多くの食べ物を見つけることができます。そのため，この時期は，彼らはそのことを心配する必要はありません。しかし，夏には別の問題があります。フロリダ周辺の海は，人々がボートを使ったり，ウォータースポーツをしたりして楽しむのに人気の場所です。これらの人々が使うボートはとても速く進むので，灰色のマナティーが水面の近くで泳いでいる時，彼らを見つけることは困難です。毎年の夏に，多くのマナティーがボートの事故で亡くなります。

フロリダの問題はとても深刻です。もしフロリダのマナティーの数が減り続けるなら，その状況を改善するのはとても難しいでしょう。マナティーは通常，一度に1頭だけ赤ん坊を産み，母親のマナティーは彼女たちの赤ん坊が生まれる前，たいてい12か月間妊娠しています。この理由のため，私たちはとても注意深くなり，フロリダのマナティーの数をチェックし続けなければなりません。

5 (1) ① 直後の「将来私は保育士になりたい」という部分は，文前半の内容の「理由」を表している。② 直後の「彼はしばしば泣いて，私に止まるように頼んだ」という文から考える。③ 聡史からスプーンを取り上げて食べさせた友紀への言葉。watch には「見守る」という意味がある。(2) 質問は「2日目に，友紀と聡史はどこにいましたか？」。第3段落の1文目を見る。彼女たちは友紀の家にいた。(3)「失敗から学べること」なので，「物事をより上手にする方法」を選ぶ。(4) A．第2段落の最終文を見る。it は “Walking slowly with little children” を指す。B．第3段落の最終文より，“listening carefully is important” に注目。C．第4段落の最終文に “helping too much is not good” とある。(5) ア．第1段落の2文目を見る。友紀が聡史と会うのは初めてのことだった。イ．第4段落の3・4文目を見る。友紀が聡史の食事を手助けしたとき，おばは悲しそうだった。ウ．「冬休み中に，友紀は聡史と多くのよい経験をした」。最終段落の1文目を見る。正しい。

【全訳】 今日は冬休み中の体験についてお話ししたいと思います。去年の12月に，おばとおじが私の家に3日間滞在し，私は彼らの息子の聡史と初めて会いました。彼はまだ2歳です。将来私は保育士になりたいと思っているので，私にとってそれは彼のような幼い子どもたちの世話をする方法を学ぶよい機会でした。

初日に，私たちは動物園へ行き，たくさんの動物を見ました。私は彼と手をつないで一緒に歩きましたが，時々私は彼にとって速く歩きすぎてしまいました。彼はしばしば泣いて，私に止まるように頼みました。私にとって，幼い子どもたちと一緒にゆっくり歩くことは少し難しかったのですが，それは彼らの世話をするときに大切なことであると気付きました。

2日目，私たちは家の中で歌を歌ったりボールで遊んだりして1日中楽しみました。一緒に遊んでいたとき，彼がよく私に話しかけてきたのですが，私は彼の言葉のいくつかを理解することができませんでした。一生懸命に彼の言葉を聞こうとすると，彼はにっこり笑ってさらに私に話しかけました。注意深く聞くことは，幼い子どもたちと意思の疎通を図るのに大切であることを私は学びました。

最後の日，私たちは一緒に昼食を食べました。聡史はうまくスプーンを使うことができず，テーブルの上に食べ物をこぼし続けました。そこで，私は彼の手からスプーンを取り，それで彼の口へ食べ物を運んであげました。私はよいことをしたと思ったのですが，おばは悲しそうな様子で，私にやめるように頼みました。彼女は「友紀，お姉さんのように聡史を助けてくれてありがとう，でも彼は全力で頑張っているの。今，彼は学んでいるところだから，ただ彼を見守ってあげてね」と言いました。何かをしようとしているときに手伝いすぎることは，幼い子どもたちにとってよいことではないと私は学びました。

彼の滞在中，私は多くのよい経験をしました。私たちにとって，たくさんの経験をしてたくさん失敗することは大切だということを私は学びました。失敗を通して，私たちは物事をより上手にする方法を学ぶことができます。私は聡史から大切なことを学びました。

6 (1) あ．プラスティック製品は自然に還らず太陽光で細かく分解され，その「結果」として，浜辺や海中に大量のマイクロプラスティックが存在する。「結果として」= as a result。い．マイクロプラスティックが健康に悪いことを述べたあとの1文。「科学者たちでさえどう悪影響を及ぼすのかわかっていない」という内容を続けるには，逆説の表現が必要。「しかしながら」= however。う．直前であげているプラスティック製品の「代わりに」水筒や買い物袋を持参することを提案している。「代わりに」= instead。(2) 1．マイクロプラスティックは「海中だけではなく空中にもある」。「AだけではなくBも」= not only A but also B。2．直後に節〈主語＋動詞〉があることに着目する。節と節をつなぐには接続詞が必要。「マイクロプラスティックは非常に小さい『けれども』，将来大きな問題を生み出すかもしれない」。「～だけれども」= though ～。3.「汚染を止めることは，たった一人の人にとっては難しいかもしれない」。「～することはAにとって…だ」= It is … for A to ～。(3)「この種のマイクロプラスティックは私たちの目で見るにはあまりに小さい」→「この種のマイクロプラスティックはとても小さいので，私たちは目で見ることはできない」。「とても～なので…」= so ～ that …。(4) ② without knowing ～ =「～を知ることなく」。thatは直前の文の内容を指している。⑥ 世界中の人々が「みんなでしたら」できること。itは直前の文のto stop the pollutionを指している。(5) 企業は何の解決法を考え始めたのか→直前で「『プラスティックの環境問題』が更に深刻になりつつある」と述べている。(6) must =「～しなければならない」。to以下は目的を表す副詞的用法の不定詞なので，「～するために」と訳す。(7) あとに “First, let's ～”，“Second, let's ～” と二つの提案が続くので，「私たちが今すぐできることが二つある」という意味の文にする。「～がある」= There are ～。「私たちができること」= things we can do。thingsのあとに目的格の関係代名詞が省略された形。「今すぐ」= right away。(8) ア．「科学者たちは彼らが調べた雨の中にマイクロプラスティックを発見した」。第1段落の2文目を見る。正しい。イ．第1段落の最後から2文目を見る。マイクロプラスティックは自然に還らない。ウ．「合成繊維は衣類によいが，北極で簡単にマイクロプラスティックになる」という記述はない。エ．「将来，科学者だけがマイクロプラスティックの影響を発見する」という記述はない。オ．「無料の箸」については述べられていない。カ．「もし世界中の人々が通りをきれいにし，自分の水筒や買い物袋を使えば，将来プラスティックの雨はおさまるかもしれない」。最終段落を見る。正しい。

【全訳】 あなたは今までに「プラスティックの雨」という言葉を聞いたことがありますか？　科学者たちが雨を調査したところ，彼らは雨水の中に非常に小さなプラスティックの欠片を発見しました。それらは90％の雨の中に見つかりました。世界中の人々はその報告を聞いて驚き，その問題に興味を持つようになりました。これらの非常に小さなプラスティックの欠片は「マイクロプラスティック」とよばれます。マイクロプラスティックは私たちの身の回りにある，実に多くのプラスティック製品から生み出されます。例えば，私たちはよく浜辺や海で漂流ごみを目にします。その中にはペットボトルやビニール袋もあります。それらは自然に還ることはなく，太陽の光で細かい欠片に分解されます。その結果として，浜辺や海中には現在，非常に多くのマイクロプラスティックが存在しています。

では，なぜ雨の中にマイクロプラスティックがあるのでしょうか？　それらは海の中だけではなく，空気の中にもあるのです！　例えば，私たちの衣類に用いられる合成繊維もプラスティック製品で，それらは簡単にマイクロプラスティックになってしまいます。この種のマイクロプラスティックはあまりに小さいので，私たちは自分の目では見ることができません。それらは風によって運ばれ，雨や雪とともに世界中の地面に落ちてきます。それらは北極でさえ見つかりました。

マイクロプラスティックは非常に小さいですが，それらは将来大きな問題を生み出すかもしれません。海の魚はマイクロプラスティックを食べ続けるかもしれません。私たちはそれを知らずにその魚を食べ続けるかもしれません。私たちは空中の大量のマイクロプラスティックを吸い込み続けるかもしれません。私たちはマイクロプラスティックが体内に入らないように気をつけなければなりません。しかしながら，科学者たちでさえ，マイクロプラスティックが私たちの健康にどのような影響を及ぼすのかわかっていないのです。

プラスティックの環境問題は更に深刻になりつつあります。世界の非常に多くの企業が，どのようにそれらを解決するかを考え始めました。無料でビニール袋を提供するのをやめるスーパーマーケットやコンビニエンスストアもあります。プラスティックのストローを使うのをやめて，紙のストローを使い始めるコーヒーショップやファストフード店もあります。

今，私たちはプラスティック汚染を止めるために何かをしなければなりません。今すぐ私たちができることが二つあります。まず，近所のプラスティックごみを拾いましょう。それはしばしば川へ流れ込み，最終的に海に至ります。もし私たちが近くの通りをきれいにすれば，私たちから遠く離れた海をきれいにすることができます。次に，ペットボトルやビニール袋などのプラスティック製品の使用を減らしましょう。代わりに，自分の水筒や買い物袋を持っていきませんか？　これらのことをして汚染を止めるのは，たった一人の人には難しいかもしれません。しかし，もし世界の人々がみんなでそれらをすれば，私たちには汚染を止めることができます。そうすれば私たちは，プラスティックの雨のない未来を見ることができるかもしれません。

7 (1) 博士が親と話すときにいつも話題に上がるもの。直後の2文で，親たちはソーシャルメディアとよばれるウェブサイトについて心配している，という内容が述べられている。(2)「多くの親は自分の子供が常にソーシャルメディア上にいると言っている」という意味の文。親との対話について述べているのは第1段落のみ。「親はそれら（ウェブサイト）が10代の若者に悪いのではないかと疑問に思っている」という文の直前に入れるのが適切。(3) show that ～=「～ということを示す」。have an effect on ～=「～に影響を与える」。(4) 第2段落ではソーシャルメディアが若者に与える悪影響について，第3段落では若者にとってのソーシャルメディアのよい点について述べている。空欄の前後の内容が対比されているので，「しかしながら」という意味の however が適切。(5) 比較級を用いて，主語の「ソーシャルメディアで友達と時間を過ごすヘビーゲーマー」と「そうしないゲーマー」を比べている。who はどちらも gamers を後ろから修飾する主格の関係代名詞。主語の who に続く部分が省略されている。(6)「A に B を与える」= give A B。「話す機会」は形容詞的用法の不定詞で表す。it can give them a chance to talk となる。(7) 直前の文で「ソーシャルメディアを使うことが一部の若者に非常に多くの問題を引き起こす」とある→「彼らは完全に『それをやめる』必要があるかもしれない」とする。(8) ア.「ペイト博士はある専門家で，困っている10代の若者を助けている」。第1段落の前半を見る。正しい。イ. 第1段落を見る。「スナップチャット」は若者が使っているウェブサイトとしてあげられている。ウ.「ソーシャルメディアで，人々はメッセージと投稿を使ってコミュニケーションをとることができる」。第1段落の後半を見る。正しい。エ.「気分が落ち込むと感じることは10代の若者に問題を引き起こすかもしれない」。第2段落を見る。正しい。オ．最終段落の後半を見る。ペイト博士はソーシャルメディアを上手に使う10代の若者もいると言っている。

【全訳】 ドリュー・ペイト博士は10代の若者についての専門家です。彼は悲しいと感じたり心配したりしている10代の若者を助けています。彼はまた彼らの親と話もします。彼が彼らと話すとき，あることがいつも話題に上がります。人々はインスタグラムやフェイスブック，スナップチャットのようなウェブサイトのことを心配しているのです。このようなウェブサイトはソーシャルメディアとよばれます。人々はメッセージと投稿を通して他人と繋がることができます。多くの親は自分の子供が常にソーシャルメディア上にいると言います。親たちはそれらが10代の若者に悪いのではないかと疑問に思っています。

科学者たちはソーシャルメディアの10代の若者への影響を明らかにしようとしています。ソーシャルメディアを使うことは若い人々に悪い影響を与えるということを示す研究がありました。それは彼らを心配させ気分を落ち込ませることもあります。人は気分が落ち込むと，幸せを感じるのが難しくなります。彼らは自分の気持ちを制御することができないかもしれません。彼らはなかなか眠れないかもしれません。

しかしながら，ソーシャルメディアを使うことは10代の若者を助けることもあると言う科学者もいます。例えば，ある研究では何時間もビデオゲームをしている10代の若者を調べました。ソーシャルメディアで友達と時間を過ごすヘビーゲーマーは，そうしないゲーマーよりも気分が落ち込んだり心配したりすることが少ないようでした。ソーシャルメディアの別のよい点が，それは彼らに自分たちの問題について話す機会を与えることができるということです。このようにして，彼らはありのままでいることができるのです。

ペイト博士は，ソーシャルメディアを使うことが一部の10代の若者に非常に多くの問題を引き起こすと言いました。彼らはそれを完全にやめる必要があるのかもしれません。ウェブサイトで費やす時間を減らせばいいだけの若者もいます。彼らは友達の小さなグループとコミュニケーションをとる必要もあるかもしれません。ソーシャルメディアを上手に使う10代の若者もいます。彼らにとって，ウェブサイトは単純に楽しいのです。「それは10代の若者ごとに異なります」とペイト博士は言いました。

2．英 作 文 （P. 28〜37）

整序作文

〈解答〉

1 （2番目・4番目の順に）(1) イ・ウ　(2) エ・イ　(3) エ・ア　(4) ウ・ア　(5) ウ・エ

2 （3番目・5番目の順に）(1) ウ・ク　(2) カ・イ　(3) オ・イ　(4) イ・ウ　(5) イ・カ

3 (1) ア　(2) オ　(3) エ　(4) オ　(5) ア　(6) イ

4 (1) ウ　(2) イ　(3) カ　(4) ア　(5) イ　(6) エ

5 (1) ア　(2) オ　(3) ア　(4) A. イ　B. ア　(5) C. カ　D. ウ

6 （A・Bの順に）(1) エ・ア　(2) カ・オ　(3) カ・キ　(4) ア・イ　(5) オ・ウ　(6) カ・ウ

7 (1) My parents don't let us watch TV after　(2) Tomorrow will not be as hot as today　(3) Whose desk do we have to carry　(4) It's not difficult for her to read English books　(5) How long have you been studying math

8 (1) looking forward to seeing　(2) It is difficult for me to read　(3) stayed at school until　(4) enough money to buy food

9 (1) You don't have to worry about that　(2) He told us not to use a dictionary　(3) Look at the broken chair　(4) The man who came to meet us was very kind

1 (1) 数をたずねる言い方は〈How many ＋〜(名詞の複数形)〉で表す。How many pens do you have in your bag?となる。(2)「私は〜するつもりだ」= I will 〜。「〜に電話をする」= call 〜。I will call him tomorrow.

となる。(3)「どちらの〜」=〈Which +〜(名詞)〉。Which picture is hers?となる。(4)「〜を聴く」= listen to 〜。「夕食後」= after dinner。I usually listen to music after dinner.となる。(5)「〜がある」= there is/are 〜。「〜の前に」= in front of 〜。There is a bookstore in front of Takumi's house.となる。

2 (1)「駅まで」を「駅に到着するために」と考え，to get to the station と表す。時間の長さをたずねる疑問詞は how long。take 〜 =「(時間が)〜かかる」。How long does it take from here to get to the station?となる。(2)「〜しませんか？」= How about 〜ing?。「散歩をする」= take a walk。How about taking a walk on Sunday?となる。(3)「観光の名所」を「訪れるべき場所」と考え，places to visit と表す。「〜がある」= there is/are 〜。There are many places to visit in Kyoto.となる。(4)「〜へ行く途中に」= on one's way to 〜。I met her on my way to school.となる。(5) 受動態〈be 動詞＋過去分詞〉の文。「〜中で」= all over 〜。This song is sung all over the world.となる。

3 (1)「〜への道を A に教える」= tell A the way to 〜。Can you tell me the way to the post office?となる。(2) which は the pen を先行詞とする目的格の関係代名詞である。That is the pen which my mother gave me.となる。(3) standing は現在分詞の形容詞的用法で，the woman を修飾する。Who is the woman standing by the window?となる。(4)「A に B を与える」= give A B。「何か熱い飲み物」= something hot to drink。Please give me something hot to drink.となる。(5)「〜に行ったことがある」= have/has been to 〜。My brother has been to Australia twice.となる。(6)「〜すぎて…できない」= too 〜 to …。Tom is too busy to help you now.となる。

4 (1) 期間をたずねる疑問詞は How long。「(あなたは)〜するつもりですか？」= are you going to 〜。How long are you going to stay in Okinawa?となる。(2)「何があなたを怒らせたのですか？」と考える。「〜を怒らせる」= make 〜 angry。What made you angry?となる。(3)「A に〜するように頼む」= ask A to 〜。I asked Ken to come with me.となる。(4)「〜とは異なる」= be different from 〜。Her idea is different from mine.となる。(5) 現在完了〈have/has ＋過去分詞〉の否定文。The soccer game has not started yet.となる。(6)「親切にも〜する」= kind enough to 〜。She was kind enough to help me.となる。

5 (1) 頻度を表す副詞は，主語と一般動詞の間に置く。My grandfather usually goes to bed at nine.となる。(2) 疑問詞の where が文頭。後は過去進行形の疑問文の語順〈was/were ＋主語＋〜ing〉。Where were you studying at eight?となる。(3)「何を言ったらよいか」= what to say。She didn't know what to say.となる。(4)「A に〜してもらいたい」= want A to 〜。「A に〜を届ける」= bring 〜 to A。I want you to bring this letter to him by tomorrow.となる。(5)「木のそばで眠っているネコ」= the cat which is sleeping by the tree。which は主格の関係代名詞で，which 以下が the cat を後ろから修飾する。Look at the cat which is sleeping by the tree.となる。

6 (1)「もう 1 つの〜」= another piece of 〜。Would you like to have another piece of cake?となる。(2)「A を〜のままにする」= leave A 〜。You should not leave the windows open at night.となる。(3) 仮定法過去の文。If I were you, I wouldn't do such a thing to her.となる。(4) 関係代名詞 that を使った文にする。Kinkaku-ji is the most beautiful temple that I've ever visited.となる。(5) 現在分詞が前にある名詞を修飾する形にする。The girl reading a book in the library is my sister.となる。(6)「どのような種類の〜」= what kind of 〜。What kind of music are you interested in?となる。

7 (1)「A に〜させる」=〈let A ＋動詞の原形〉。(2)「A ほど〜ない」= not as 〜 as A　(3) have/has to 〜の疑問文。〈do/does ＋主語＋ have to 〜〉となる。(4)「A が〜するのは…だ」= It's … for A to 〜。(5) 現在完了進行形の疑問文。〈have/has ＋主語＋ been ＋動詞の ing 形〉。「どれくらいの間」= how long。

8 (1)「〜することを楽しみにする」= look forward to 〜ing。(2)「A にとって〜することは…である」= it is … for A to 〜。(3)「〜にいる」= stay at 〜。「〜まで」= until 〜。(4)「〜するのに十分なお金」= enough money to 〜。この場合 enough「十分な」は形容詞で，名詞の前に置く。

9 (1)「～する必要はない」= don't/doesn't have to ～。「～について心配する」= worry about ～。(2)「A に～しないように言う」= tell A not to ～。(3)「壊れた椅子」= broken chair。過去分詞 1 語の場合は，名詞を前から修飾する。(4)「私たちを迎えに来てくれた男性」= the man who came to meet us。who は主格の関係代名詞で，who came to meet us が the man を後ろから修飾する。

自由英作文

〈解答〉

10 （例）Whose notebook is it

11 （例）② I'm looking for my bag（または，I can't find my bag など） ⑥ Where did you buy it（または，How did you get it など） ⑨ Have you ever been to Australia（または，Have you seen koalas before など）

12 （例）(1) The woman will go to the supermarket to buy some eggs.（11 語） (2) is reading a book under ／ are playing volleyball by

13 （例 1）A girl looks sad because it is raining. （例 2）A girl hopes that it will stop raining.

14 （例）(1) I enjoyed my school trip the best (2) I took many pictures with my classmates

15 （例）(1) we can see many kinds of clothes in a short time.（11 語） (2) we can ask some questions about them and we can also try them on.（14 語）

16 （例）(1) ① I cooked dinner for my family. ② It was fun to cook for someone. (2) We can see many beautiful flowers here in each season.（10 語）

17 （例 1）French ／ I hear the sounds of French are the most beautiful of all languages. Everyone who can speak it looks cool.（20 語） （例 2）Korean ／ I'm interested in Korean music. I want to understand the words and sing the songs of my favorite singer.（19 語）

18 A. playing sports B. playing soccer with my friends is fun

10 生徒が「それは私のものです」と答えていることから，ノートの持ち主を尋ねる疑問文を作る。「誰のノート」= whose notebook。

11 ② アンの「何をしているのですか？」という質問に対する返答。アンの「ああ，それなら体育館で見ました」という言葉やバッグの絵から考える。「僕はバッグを探しています」，「バッグが見つからないのです」などの文が入る。⑥ 春樹の「オーストラリアで手に入れました」という返答から考える。「あなたはそれをどこで買ったのですか？」，「あなたはどうやってそれを手に入れたのですか？」などの文が入る。⑨ 二人がコアラについて話している場面。アンの「いいえ，ありません。私は将来，そこに行って彼らを見たいです」という返答から考える。「あなたは今までにオーストラリアに行ったことがありますか？」，「あなたは以前にコアラを見たことがありますか？」などの文が入る。「あなたは今までに～に行ったことがありますか？」= Have you ever been to ～?。

12 (1) 女性は卵を買うためにスーパーマーケットに行こうと考えている。未来時制は will や be going to で表す。「～するために」と目的を表すには不定詞〈to ＋動詞の原形〉を用いる。(2) 少女は木の下で本を読んでいる。2 人の少年は木のそばでバレーボールをしている。ともに現在進行形〈be 動詞＋～ing〉を用いて説明する。under ～＝「～の下で」。by ～＝「～のそばで」。

13 女の子が外の雨を見て悲しそうにしている。〈look ＋～(形容詞)〉＝「～に見える」。「雨が降っている」は現在進行形〈be 動詞＋～ing〉で表す。てるてる坊主から女の子は雨が止むのを願っている様子もわかる。

14 (1) 中学校生活で最も楽しんだことについて英作する。(2) (1)で答えたことについて，どのようなことをしたのか，どのように感じたのかなどについて述べる。

15 (1) インターネットで衣類を買うことが便利な理由を書く。「いろんな種類の服を短時間で見ることができるから」や「店に行く必要がないから」などが考えられる。(2) 実際に店に行って衣類を買う方が良い理由を書く。「衣服について店員にたずねることができるから」や「試着できるから」などが考えられる。

16 (1) ①「家族のために夕食を作った」,「海へ泳ぎに行った」,「家族と北海道に行った」など，一般動詞の過去形を用いて文を作る。②「だれかのために料理をするのは楽しかった」などのように，感想を具体的に述べる。(2)「季節ごとにたくさんのきれいな花を見ることができる」,「私たちが楽しむことのできる行事がたくさんある」など，直後の「だから私たちは自分たちの学校が大好きです」という1文につながる英文を作る。

17 「フランス語」を選択した解答例は，「私はフランス語の音がすべての言語の中で最も美しいと聞いています。それを話すことができる人はだれもかっこいいです」。I hear ～＝「私は～と聞いている」。「韓国語」を選択した解答例は，「私は韓国の音楽に興味があります。言葉を理解して，お気に入りの歌手の歌を歌いたいです」。I'm interested in ～＝「私は～に興味がある」。

18 解答例は「『友だちとサッカーをするのが楽しい』ので，私は『スポーツをすること』の方がよりおもしろいと思います」。「スポーツをみること」＝ watching sports。

3．英 文 法 (P. 40～47)

英文完成選択

〈解答〉

1 (1) イ (2) ウ (3) イ (4) イ (5) ア (6) ウ (7) ウ (8) ア (9) ウ (10) イ
2 (1) イ (2) ウ (3) イ (4) ア (5) ウ
3 (1) イ (2) イ (3) ウ (4) イ
4 (1) ウ (2) イ (3) エ (4) ウ (5) イ (6) エ (7) イ (8) ア (9) ア (10) エ
5 (1) イ (2) エ (3) ウ (4) ア (5) ウ
6 (1) ウ (2) イ (3) ア (4) ウ (5) エ (6) ア (7) ウ (8) ウ (9) ウ (10) イ

1 (1)「私の町には見るべきたくさんの場所がある」。「～がある」＝ there is (are) ～。あとに複数形が続くのでare を選ぶ。(2)「あなたはどちらがより好きですか，コーヒーですか，それとも紅茶ですか？」。「どちらが」＝which。(3)「私は友達からよくユミと呼ばれる」。受動態の文なので過去分詞を選ぶ。(4)「もし，明日雨が降れば，私たちはハイキングに行かないだろう」。「もし～なら」＝ if ～。(5)「私の兄（弟）は6年間サッカーをしている」。「～の間」＝ for ～。(6)「私は家族の中で最も背が高い」。最上級の文なので tallest を選ぶ。(7)「このケーキは彼のものです」。「彼のもの」＝ his。(8)「私のために窓を開けてもらえませんか？」。「～してもらえませんか？」＝ Will you ～?。(9)「彼女はその知らせを聞いて，うれしそうに見えた」。原因を表す不定詞の副詞的用法。(10)「彼がどこに住んでいるか私は知りません。私に彼の住所を教えてください」。「どこに」＝ where。

2 (1)「急ぎなさい，さもなければ電車に乗り遅れるよ」。「～しなさい，さもなければ…」＝〈～(命令文), or …〉。(2)「それは私のものである」。「私のもの」＝ mine。(3)「私はケーキを作るのが得意だ」。「～することが得意だ」＝ be good at ～ing。(4)「あなたは今までに北海道へ行ったことがありますか？」。現在完了の経験用法の疑問文なので have で始まる。(5)「2月は1年の『2番目の』月である」。

3 (1) 関係代名詞を用いた文。先行詞 the picture は物なので，which が適切。「私がオーストラリアで撮った写真をあなたにお見せしましょう」。(2) both A and B ＝「A も B も」。「トムもケンも今サッカーをしています」。(3) enjoy ～ing ＝「～するのを楽しむ」。「人々は野球の試合を見るのを楽しみました」。(4) 主語が三人称単数で現在の文なので，has が適切。「すべての子どもがさまざまな夢を持っています」。

4 (1)「アンディは昨日，リンゴを食べました」。yesterday があるので過去形の文。(2)「あなたのペンを使ってもいいですか？」―「もちろんです。はい，どうぞ」。「～してもいいですか？」＝ May I ～?。(3)「私の夢は先生になることです」。「～すること」は不定詞〈to ＋動詞の原形〉で表すことができる。(4)「木の下に立っているその少年は私の弟です」。「～している」は現在分詞を用いて表すことができる。(5)「私は今，部屋の掃除をしなければなりません」。助動詞のあとの動詞は原形になる。(6)「ルーシーはクラスで最も背の高い少女です」。直前の the に注目。最上級の文。(7)「私にとって歌うことはとても楽しいです」。「～すること」は動名詞を用いて表すことができる。(8)「この巨大な寺院はいつ建てられたのですか？」。「～された」は受動態〈be 動詞＋過去分詞〉の過去形の文で表す。(9)「これは私が先週買ったバッグです」。目的格の関係代名詞を用いて the bag を後ろから修飾する。先行詞が「もの」の場合は which か that を用いる。(10)「ケンタとニックは，私がここに着いたときからずっとテニスをしています」。動作の継続は現在完了進行形〈have been ＋～ing〉で表す。

5 (1)「私は今日するべき宿題がたくさんある」。homework は不可算名詞なので複数形にはならない。また，many は可算名詞を，much は不可算名詞を，a lot of は両方を修飾する。(2)「昨夜私が両親を訪ねたとき，彼らは夕食を食べていた」。「～していた」は過去進行形〈be 動詞の過去形＋～ing〉で表す。(3)「トムはサッカーをするのが本当に得意だ」。「～するのが得意だ」= be good at ～ing。(4)「あなたは今までに東京スカイツリーに行ったことがありますか？」。「～に行ったことがある」= have been to ～。経験を表す現在完了。(5)「富士山は日本の他のどの山よりも高い」。「他のどの～よりも」=〈than any other ＋～(単数名詞)〉。

6 (1)「彼は 3 年間ずっとサッカーをしています」。現在完了進行形〈have/has been ＋～ing〉の文。(2)「もし私が鳥なら，あなたのところに飛んでいけるのに」。現在の事実とは異なることは，仮定法〈if ＋主語＋動詞の過去形，主語＋助動詞の過去形＋動詞の原形〉で表す。if 節の be 動詞には were が好まれる。(3)「この薬はあなたをぐっすり眠らせてくれるでしょう」。〈make ＋人＋動詞の原形〉=「人を～させる」。(4)「私が彼の電話番号を知っていたらいいのになぁ」。現実とは異なる願望を表す仮定法の文。wish に続く節の動詞には過去形を用いる。(5)「トムは自分の部屋を掃除し終わりました」。「～し終える」= finish ～ing。(6)「彼と私は 2 匹の犬を飼っています」。主語が複数のとき，現在形は動詞の原形となる。(7)「あそこに立っているあの男の子をごらんなさい」。「～している」は現在分詞で表す。standing 以下が後ろから that boy を修飾する形。(8)「ジョンは 10 歳です。ケンは 11 歳です。ジョンはケンより年下です」。比較級の文。(9)「私には東京に住んでいる友人がいます」。a friend を先行詞とした主格の関係代名詞が入る。(10)「あなたは今日学校へ行く必要がありません。今日は日曜日だからです」。「～する必要がない」= don't have to ～。

同意文完成

〈解答〉

7 (1) by，car (2) have，time (3) teaches，us (4) older，than (5) has，been

8 (1) my (2) Let's (3) Don't (4) no (5) are，in

9 (1) Did，help (2) It，to (3) There，are（または，we，have） (4) most，of (5) gone，to

10 (1) by，taxi (2) had，could（または，would） (3) who（または，that），is (4) how，important (5) swims，better

11 (1) If，don't (2) There，are (3) which（または，that），has (4) of，them (5) biggest，ever

7 (1)「あなたは車を運転して仕事に行きますか？」→「あなたは車で仕事へ行きますか？」。「(交通手段の)～で」= by ～。(2)「私は今日忙しいので，あなたに会うことができない」→「私は今日あなたに会うための時間がない」。不定詞の形容詞的用法。(3)「彼は私たちの英語の先生だ」→「彼は私たちに英語を教える」。(4)「アキラはヒロシほど年をとっていない」=「ヒロシはアキラより年上だ」。(5)「昨日雨が降り始めて，今もまだ降っている」→「昨日からずっと雨が降っている」。現在完了進行形の〈have (has) ＋ been ＋～ing 形〉にする。

8 (1)「このコンピューターは私のものです」→「これは私のコンピューターです」。「私の」= my。(2)「買い物に行きましょうか？」→「買い物に行きましょう」。「～しましょう」= let's ～。(3)「英語の授業で日本語を話してはいけません」→「英語の授業で日本語を話すな」。「～するな」= Don't ～。(4)「その公園にはだれもいませんでした」。「1 人もない，1 つもない」= no。(5)「私の町には 3 つの公園があります」。「～がある」= there is/are

〜。「〜の町に」= in one's town。

9 (1) 受動態の文を能動態に書きかえる。「その犬はあなたを助けましたか？」。(2)「バイオリンを弾くことは私にとって楽しい」。「A にとって…することは〜である」= it is 〜 for A to …。(3)「1 年には 12 か月ある」。「〜がある」= there is (are) 〜。後に複数形が続くので be 動詞は are にする。なお，we have 〜でも可。(4)「イギリスでは，サッカーは他のどのスポーツよりも人気がある」→「イギリスでは，サッカーはすべてのスポーツの中で最も人気がある」。(5)「彼女は先月パリへ行って，今ここにはいない」→「彼女はパリへ行ってしまった」。現在完了の結果用法。

10 (1)「私は美術館までタクシーに乗りました」→「私はタクシーで美術館に行きました」。「〜(乗り物)で」= by 〜。(2)「私は十分な時間がないので，山の寺を訪問することができません」→「十分な時間があれば，山の寺を訪問できる（する）のに」。仮定法〈If ＋主語＋動詞の過去形，主語＋助動詞の過去形(could/would)＋動詞の原形〜〉。(3)「あなたは向こうで写真を撮っている少女を知っていますか？」。現在分詞の後置修飾の文を，主格の関係代名詞を使って書きかえる。(4)「彼らは手をきれいにしておくことの重要性を理解していません」→「彼らは手をきれいにしておくことがどれくらい大切か理解していません」。「どれくらい大切か」= how important。it は形式主語で，to 以下の内容を指す。(5)「ケンは私たちのクラスの中で最も上手な泳者です」→「ケンは私たちのクラスの他のどの生徒より上手に泳ぎます」。最上級の内容を比較級で書きかえる。「他のどの〜より」= than any other 〜。

11 (1)「あなたの助けがなければ私はこの仕事を終えることができません」→「もしあなたが私を助けてくれなければ，私はこの仕事を終えることができません」。「もしあなたが〜しなければ」= if you don't 〜。(2)「この都市には訪れるべき場所がたくさんあります」。「〜がたくさんある」= there are many 〜。(3)「私は犬を飼っています。それは青い目をしています」→「私は青い目をした犬を飼っています」。主格の関係代名詞を用いて表す。先行詞が動物の場合は which (または，that)を用いる。(4)「彼らはみんな高校生です」。「彼らはみんな」= all of them。(5)「私は東京のように大きな都市を訪れたことがありません」→「東京は私がこれまでに訪れた最も大きな都市です」。最上級を用いた表現。「私がこれまでに〜した」= I've ever 〜。

正誤判断

〈解答〉

12 (1) ア　(2) ウ　(3) ア　(4) ア　(5) ウ

13 (1) エ　(2) イ　(3) ウ　(4) イ　(5) ア

14 (1) イ　(2) エ　(3) エ　(4) ア

15 (記号，訂正の順に) (1) エ，been　(2) イ，were taken　(3) イ，making　(4) ウ，〔who is〕standing　(5) ア，at

12 (1) if でくくられた節の中の動詞は，未来を表す場合も現在形にする。(2) 動詞が looks と三単現の形なので，付加疑問文には don't ではなく doesn't を使う。(3)「あなたは中国にどれくらい滞在するつもりですか？」。期間をたずねる疑問文なので，疑問詞は how much ではなく how long を使う。(4) 助動詞 can の後の動詞は原形になる。(5)「あなたはオーストラリアで使われる言語を知っていますか？」。過去分詞を使った文なので，using ではなく used を使う。

13 (1) 形容詞的用法の不定詞なので，drinking ではなく drink が正しい。(2) give 〜 …＝「〜に…をあげる」なので，gave him a watch が正しい。または，gave a watch to him でもよい。(3) 先行詞が人なので，which ではなく who が正しい。(4) rain は数えられない名詞なので，many ではなく much が正しい。(5)「公園で」と答えているので，when ではなく where が正しい。

14 (1) feel 〜＝「〜のように感じる」。「〜」は形容詞が入るので sadly ではなく sad が正しい。(2)「オカダ氏によって書かれたこの本はあなたには興味深いですか」という意味の文。interested ではなく interesting が正しい。(3)「これは私が今までに見た最も美しい花です」という意味の文。never ではなく ever を使う。(4)「横浜での私の滞在中に」。接続詞の while ではなく前置詞の during を使う。

15 (1)「私は USJ へ行ったことがない」。have never been to ～＝「～へ行ったことがない」。(2)「これらの写真は約 30 年前に祖父によって撮られた」。受動態〈be 動詞＋過去分詞〉の形にする。(3)「その大きな音を立てるのをやめてもらえませんか？」。stop ～ing ＝「～するのをやめる」。(4)「門の前に立っている女性」。現在分詞 standing を使う。(5) 時刻の前につく前置詞は in ではなく at。

語形変化

〈解答〉

16 (1) said　(2) were　(3) hotter　(4) singing　(5) raining

17 (記号，正しい形の順に) (1) オ，chosen　(2) イ，is　(3) エ，written　(4) カ，had　(5) ウ，arriving

16 (1)「私が教室を出たとき，カトウ先生は私に何かを言いました」。when ～＝「～するとき」。when ～が過去の文なので過去形にする。(2)「ケンと私は昨日の午前中図書館にいました」。主語は「ケンと私」なので複数。複数の過去を表す be 動詞は were。(3)「このスープはあれより熱いです」。比較級の形にする。t を重ねることに注意。(4)「私はその歌っている少女をとてもよく知っています」。「歌っている」なので現在分詞が girl を修飾する形にする。(5)「昨夜雨がやみました」。stop ～ing ＝「～するのをやめる，～するのがとまる」。

17 (1)「バスケットボールクラブのメンバーの中で，誰がキャプテンとして『選ばれ』ましたか？」。受動態〈be 動詞＋過去分詞〉の疑問文。「選ぶ」＝ choose。(2)「ブライアンは今，家にいません。彼が戻ったら，あなたが訪ねてきたと彼に伝えましょう」。時を表す副詞節では，未来のことは現在形で表す。(3)「先生は夏目漱石によって『書かれた』坊ちゃんという本を私に見せました」。過去分詞の後置修飾。(4)「新しいスマートフォンを買うための十分なお金を持っていたらなあ」。仮定法の文。I wish に続く現在の願望は，過去形で表す。(5)「午前 10 時に『到着する』電車はあなたをそこに時間通りに連れていくでしょう」。「～に到着する」＝ arrive at ～。現在分詞の後置修飾。

指示による文の書きかえ

〈解答〉

18 (1) Do you have to go to the post office?　(2) Miki is not as old as Taro.　(3) How long (または，How many years) has Mr. Smith lived in Osaka?　(4) There are 24 hours in a day.

19 (1) What did your brother drink for breakfast?　(2) Whose book is this?　(3) This book was written by a famous novelist.　(4) Yukiko could (または，was able to) play the violin.

18 (1) 一般動詞の現在形の疑問文。主語が you の場合は文頭に Do を置く。(2)「ミキはタロウほど歳をとっていない」と考える。「～ほど歳をとっていない」＝ not as old as ～。(3)「どれくらいの間スミスさんは大阪に住んでいますか？」という文にする。期間（年数）を尋ねる疑問詞は how long (または，how many years)。(4)「1 日の中には 24 時間あります」と考える。「～(複数)がある」＝ There are ～。

19 (1)「あなたのお兄さんは朝食に何を飲みましたか？」という過去の疑問文にする。(2)「これはだれの本ですか？」という疑問文にする。「だれの～」＝ whose ～。(3)「この本は有名な作家によって書かれた」。〈be 動詞の過去形＋過去分詞〉になる。(4) can の過去形は could。

4．会 話 文 (P. 52〜59)

〈解答〉

1 (1) ① カ ⑤ エ ⑧ ア (2) (2番目) イ (5番目) ウ (3) ③ How, about ④ already ⑥ hobby ⑦ likes, driving (4) ウ・キ

2 (1) エ (2) カ (3) ケ (4) ア (5) オ

3 (1) エ (2) カ (3) オ (4) ア (5) キ (6) イ

4 (1) A. イ B. オ C. ウ D. エ E. ア (2) イ (3) ア (4) ウ・オ

5 (1) イ (2) A. エ B. ア C. ウ (3) 一般的なマーケットは地元の食べ物や買い物を楽しんだりする場所であるが，トレインナイトマーケットは美しい夜景も楽しむことができる。(同意可) (4) a beautiful night view (5) (例) That's too bad. (6) イ・オ

6 (1) A. ア B. ウ C. ア (2) ⓐ イ ⓑ エ ⓒ ウ (3) イ，ア，オ，ウ，エ (4) (例) Are you free next Sunday? (5) understand Japanese culture

1 (1) ① 店員が客を迎えるときは，通常，最初に May I help you?とあいさつをする。⑤ 相手の言っていることを了解したと意思表示するときは，I see.を用いる。⑧ 買い物をしていて「〜を買います」と言うときは，I'll take 〜.を用いる。(2) I'd は I would の短縮形である。「〜したいと思う」= would like to 〜。buy A for B で「B に A を買う」という意味。I'd like to buy a birthday present for my father.となる。(3) ③「〜はどうですか？」= How about 〜?。④「すでに」= already。⑥「趣味」= hobby。⑦「〜するのが好きだ」= like 〜ing。drive は語尾の e をとって ing をつける。(4) ア．女性は「私は父に誕生日プレゼントを買いたいと思っています」と話している。イ．女性は「私は彼に何をあげればいいか決めることができません」と話している。ウ．店員は最初に「このネクタイはいかがですか？」と女性に薦めたので正しい。エ．店員は「私たちの店にはたくさんのものがございます」と言っており，またネクタイの次にサングラスを女性に薦めていることから，ネクタイしかないというのは誤り。オ．女性は店員に「彼はほとんどネクタイを使わないと思います」と話している。カ．女性は店員にネクタイを薦められたが，「父親はほとんどネクタイを使わないと思います」と言って断っている。キ．女性は店員が薦めたサングラスを見て，「それはとても素敵ですね！ それを買います」と言ったので正しい。

【全訳】

店員：いらっしゃいませ。

女性：はい，お願いします。私は父に誕生日プレゼントを買いたいと思っているのですが，彼に何をあげればいいか決めることができません。何か素敵なものを薦めてもらえますか？

店員：承知しました。私たちの店にはたくさんのものがございます。このネクタイはいかがでしょうか？

女性：それは素敵です，でも私の父はすでに退職しています。ですから，彼はほとんどネクタイを使わないと思います。

店員：わかりました。では，そうですね…。あなたのお父様についておたずねしてもよろしいでしょうか？

女性：はい。

店員：お父様のご趣味は何でしょうか？

女性：彼は車を運転するのが好きです。

店員：では，このサングラスはいかがでしょうか？ あなたのお父様が車を運転されているとき，これは役に立つと思います。

女性：それはとても素敵ですね！ それを買います。

店員：どうもありがとうございます。

2 (1)「どこで昼食を食べようか？」に対して，場所を提案する文が入る。空所後がピリオドで終わっているので，ケは当てはまらない。(2)「それはいい考えだけど」に続く文なので，メイが提案した場所に否定的な内容が入る。crowded =「(場所が人で）混んでいる」。(3)「それなら，あなたに何か考えがある？」に対して，別の場所を提案する文が入る。空所後がクエスチョンマークで終わっているので，ケが当てはまる。(4) 空所後に「でもマイクがそこ（レストラン）はとてもいいと言っていた」とあることから，「自分もそこに行ったことがない」と言ったことがわかる。(5)「彼（マイク）は多くのレストランで食事をしたことがあるので」に続く文なので，マイクの発言を肯定する内容が入る。

【全訳】

ボブ：どこで昼食を食べようか？

メイ：そうね，私は駅の前の新しいレストランを試したいわ。

ボブ：ああ，それはいい考えだけど，この時間は混んでいると思うよ。

メイ：ええ，たぶんそうね。それなら，あなたに何か考えがある？

ボブ：あのカフェテリアはどう？

メイ：とてもよさそうね！　私は一度もそこに行ったことがないわ。

ボブ：ぼくもそこに一度も行ったことがないけど，マイクがそれはとてもいいと言っていたよ。

メイ：彼は多くのレストランで食事をしたことがあるから，それはとてもよいでしょうね。

ボブ：よし，それなら急ごう。ぼくは空腹だよ！

3 (1) 直後に「それはとても重そうだ」とある。エを入れると，It = this book となる。また，次のケイトの発言に，「私はその本から日本の寺についてたくさん学ぶことができる」とあるので，本について触れている選択肢を入れる。(2) カメラが必要だと言うケイトへの応答。写真を撮るのが上手なケイトに，「もちろん，それ（カメラ）を持っていくべきだ」と答える文が適切。(3) 写真を撮ることについて話している。直後にユキは賛同しているので，写真を撮ることのよい点が入ると考える。(4) 同じ発言でユキは傘は必要ないと言っているので，旅行中は天気がいいと考えられる。(5) ケイトは旅行にセーターは必要ないと考えており，その理由が述べられていると考える。(6) ケイトは，ユキのお母さんがもっといいかばんを持っていると聞いて，かばんを貸してくれるよう頼むと考えられる。

【全訳】（ケイトと彼女のホストシスターであるユキがケイトの部屋で話している）

ユキ　：明日の旅行の準備はしたの，ケイト？

ケイト：まだよ。もしあなたが荷造りが終わったなら，私を手伝ってくれる？

ユキ　：ええ。見せて…。まあ，あなたはたくさんの物を持っていきたいのね。この本を持っていく必要があるの？　それはとても重そうよ。

ケイト：私たちはたくさんの有名な寺を訪れる予定なのよね？　私はその本から日本の寺についてたくさん学ぶことができるわ。それから…私はカメラも必要ね。

ユキ　：もちろん，あなたはそれを持っていくべきよ。あなたは写真を撮るのが上手だもの。

ケイト：ありがとう。私は旅行中にたくさんの写真を撮るつもりよ。

ユキ　：それはいいわね。それらは私たちにとっていい思い出になるわ。

ケイト：私もそう思う。私はあなたとあなたの家族にそれらの何枚かをあげるつもりよ。

ユキ　：ありがとう，ケイト。えっと，あなたは傘は必要ないわ。私は天気予報をチェックしたの。旅行中はいい天気よ。

ケイト：じゃあ，私はセーターが必要ないってことね？　1週間ずっと温かいわ。

ユキ　：でも明日からはとても寒くなるわ。それは持っていった方がいいわ。

ケイト：わかったわ。あら，私のかばんは小さすぎる。あなたのかばんを借りてもいい？

ユキ　：もちろんよ，でも私のお母さんがもっといいのを持っているわ。

ケイト：本当？　彼女にそれを私に貸してくれるよう頼んでみるわ。ありがとう，ユキ。

4 (1) A. 料理について尋ねている。お母さんはケーキを焼いているので，「とてもいいにおいがする」が適切。B. 直後でお母さんが「はい」と答えている。お母さんはケーキもマフィンも焼いたので，デビーは，「忙しかったでしょう？」と尋ねた。C. マフィンに気がついたデビーに，お母さんがそれはジェフのためだから，「触らないで」と言っている。D. 2つ目のアンダーソン夫人の発言に you can relax and enjoy life とある。それを受けて，デビーは「バナナケーキを1切れ食べてもいい？」と言った後に，「私は今すぐ生活を楽しみたいの」と言った。E. 直前の Your dad loves pie.に注目。Me, too.を入れると，I love pie, too.という意味で自然につながる。(2) relief =「安心」。感嘆文の主語と動詞が省略された形。デビーは心配していたテストがうまくいって安心した様子。(3) go ahead.=「はい，どうぞ」。「今それ（＝バナナケーキ）を食べていい？」に対する応答なので，「食べていいですよ」の意味。(4) ア. 2つ目のアンダーソン夫人の発言を見る。デビーはテストのためにとても一生懸命に勉強した。イ. 4つ目のアンダーソン夫人の発言を見る。マフィンはジェフのためのもの。ウ.「デビーが家に帰ったとき，お母さんはバナナケーキを作っていた」。3つ目のアンダーソン夫人の発言を見る。正しい。エ. 4つ目のアンダーソン夫人の発言を見る。アンダーソン夫人はデビーに，マフィンはジェフのものと説明しており，デビーがマフィンを食べたという記述はない。オ.「アンダーソン夫人は今日の料理のウェブサイトに投稿された新しいレシピに挑戦したいと思っている」。最後のアンダーソン夫人の発言を見る。正しい。

【全訳】

デビー　　　　　：お母さん，ただいま。

アンダーソン夫人：学校はどうだった？　テストはどうだった？

デビー　　　　　：学校は大丈夫だったし，テストもよくできた。お母さん，私はとてもそのテストのことが心配だったんだけど，今はとても気分がいいわ。ああ，安心した！

アンダーソン夫人：それを聞いてうれしいわ。あなたはここ数週間とても一生懸命に勉強していたわね。さあ，リラックスして生活を楽しむことができるわね。

デビー　　　　　：何を料理しているの？　とてもいいにおいがする。

アンダーソン夫人：ケーキを焼いているのよ。これはあなたの大好きなバナナケーキよ。

デビー　　　　　：とてもおいしそう。向こうにマフィンも見えるわ。忙しかったでしょうね？

アンダーソン夫人：ええ。ジェフが明日学校に何かを持っていかないといけないの。だから，それらのマフィンは彼のためよ。それらに触らないでね。

デビー　　　　　：バナナケーキを1切れ食べてもいい？　私は今すぐ生活を楽しみたいの。

アンダーソン夫人：夕食後まで待ちたくないの？

デビー　　　　　：それは魅力的に見えるし，きっとおいしいわ。ええ，私は待ちたくないの。今それを食べていい，お母さん？

アンダーソン夫人：いいわ，どうぞ。

デビー　　　　　：今日の料理のウェブサイトに投稿された新しいレシピを見た？　それはハワイアンパイと呼ばれていたと思うわ。

アンダーソン夫人：いいえ，見ていないわ。でも私はそのレシピに挑戦してみたいわ。あなたのお父さんはパイが大好きだもの。

デビー　　　　　：私もよ。

5 (1) Long time no see.は直訳すると「長い間会っていませんね」という意味である。(2) A. 次にソフィーが「私は元気よ，ありがとう」と答えていることから，マシューが “How have you been?” と同じ意味の質問を返したことがわかる。B. 次にソフィーが「バンコクのトレインナイトマーケットが私の一番のお気に入りだった」と答えていることから考える。C. ソフィーが「トレインナイトマーケットに美しい夜景がある」と言ったが，「マーケット」と「夜景」が結びつかずにマシューが発した言葉。(3) ソフィーの4番目のせりふを見る。1文目が「一般的なマーケット」，2文目が「トレインナイトマーケット」の説明にあたる。(4)「なぜ高い建物に行く必要があるのですか？」という質問。ソフィーの4・5番目のせりふを見る。高い所から見下ろすとマーケットの「美しい夜景」を楽しむことができると説明している。(5)「お気の毒に」= That's too bad.。(6) ア. マシューの最初のせりふを見る。マシューは「夏休みの間に君が外国へ行ったと聞いた」と言っている。イ.「世界中の多くの人々はイーペン祭をランタン祭りとして知っている」。マシューの5番目のせりふを見る。正しい。ウ. ソフィーの6・7番目のせりふを見る。ソフィーは8月にタイを訪れたので，毎年10月と11月の間に開催されるイーペン祭には参加できなかった。エ. ソフィーのおじはバンコクの旅行会社に勤めてはいるが，彼に会うことがソフィーの旅行の目的だったとは言っていない。オ.「ソフィーとマシューは将来，一緒に外国を旅行したいと思っている」。それぞれの最後のせりふを見る。正しい。

【全訳】

ソフィー：こんにちは，マシュー。ひさしぶり！　どうしていたの？

マシュー：元気だったよ。君は？　夏休みの間に君は海外へ行ったそうだね。

ソフィー：私は元気よ，ありがとう。私はタイへ行って，たくさんの有名な場所を訪れたの。

マシュー：僕はタイへ行ったことはないけれど，いつか行きたいと思っている。君にとってタイで最も素晴らしい場所はどこだった？

ソフィー：バンコクのトレインナイトマーケットが私の一番のお気に入りだったわ。タイにはたくさんのマーケットがあって，外国人訪問客にとても人気があるの。

マシュー：君の言う通りだね。でも，なぜトレインナイトマーケットが君の一番のお気に入りだったの？　他のマーケットとは何が違うんだい？

ソフィー：マーケットは品物を買ったり，地元の食べ物を食べたりすることを楽しむおもしろい場所よ。でも，トレインナイトマーケットには美しい夜景があるから，少し違っているの。

マシュー：美しい夜景？　僕にはそれが想像できないよ，だってマーケットなんだから。

ソフィー：それを見るために，あなたは高い建物へ行く必要があるわ。そうすれば，そこからマーケットの屋台の屋根をたくさん見下ろすことができて，その屋根の形は四角に見えるの。光で照らされると，屋根はたくさんの四角い宝石のようにも見えるのよ。

マシュー：わあ。それはおもしろそうだね。もし僕がいつかそこへ行くなら，カメラを持っていってその景色の写真を撮るよ。ところで，君は滞在中にイーペン祭に参加した？　その祭りはランタン祭りとして世界中の多くの人々に知られているね。そこでも素晴らしい景色を楽しむことができるよ。

ソフィー：バンコクの旅行会社に勤めている私のおじがそのことについて教えてくれたけれど，私はそれに参加することができなかったわ。

マシュー：どうしてできなかったの？

ソフィー：その祭りは毎年，10月と11月の間に開催されるけれど，私の旅行は8月だったの。

マシュー：それは残念だね。次回，君は行くべきだよ。とにかく，世界には，とてもたくさんの訪れるべき国や場所があるね。それらを調べて，僕たちが訪れたい場所のリストを作ろう。おそらく，将来，僕たちはリストにあるすべての場所を一緒に旅することができるよ。

ソフィー：ええ。私はそれが待ち切れないわ。

6 (1) A. 京子からの年賀状がとてもきれいだったから，ホストファミリー全員に見せたというジュディの言葉を聞いて京子は喜んでいる。I'm glad to hear ～=「私は～を聞いてうれしい」。B. ジュディのホストファミリーがジュディに和紙に関する興味深いビデオを見せてくれたと聞いて，京子はそれについてもっと詳しく話してほしいと思っている。C. ジュディの「あなたが自分で和紙を作ったということ？」というせりふに対する返答。(2) ⓐ「いろいろな～」= a variety of ～。ⓑ「日本の長い歴史を『学ぶ』ことができるから，和紙は大切だ」という意味になる。ⓒ 直後のI wereから仮定法の文ということがわかる。「もし私が～だったら」= if I were ～。(3)「どのようにすれば素敵な年賀状を作ることができるのかということを考えるのは楽しかった」という意味になる。「～を考えるのは楽しかった」= it was fun to think about ～。「どのようにすれば私が～できるか」= how I could ～。It was fun to think about how I could create a great *nengajo.*となる。(4)「次の日曜日は暇ですか？」などの文が入る。「暇だ」= be free。(5) 空欄を含む文は「彼女の年賀状は私たちがとてもよく『日本文化を理解する』手助けをしてくれたと思う」という意味になる。京子の4番目のせりふを利用する。

【全訳】（冬休みのあと，ジュディと京子が学校で話しています）

ジュディ：新年のあいさつ状である年賀状をありがとう。とてもきれいだったから，ホストファミリー全員にそれを見せたのよ。

京子　　：私はそれを聞いてうれしいわ。それは和紙とよばれる伝統的な日本の紙から作られているのよ。

ジュディ：私は和紙が好きなの，そしてホストファミリーが私にそれに関する興味深いビデオを見せてくれたの。

京子　　：ビデオ？　もっと私に教えて。

ジュディ：そのビデオは正倉院にある古い紙の書類についてのものだった。その紙の書類は約1,300年前に和紙から作られたの。人々はその時から和紙を使っているのよ。

京子　　：それはとても長い期間ね！　それは知らなかったわ。

ジュディ：和紙に書かれたいろいろな情報を読めば，私たちは過去の生活に関することを知ることができるわ。

京子　　：なるほど。日本の長い歴史を学ぶことができるから和紙は大切なのね？　私は一度もそのことについて考えたことがなかった。日本文化をより理解することができてうれしいわ。

ジュディ：ところで，あなたはどこであのきれいなはがきを手に入れたの？

京子　　：歴史博物館でそれを作ったのよ。

ジュディ：あなたが自分で和紙を作ったということ？

京子　　：その通り。私は小さいサイズの和紙を作り，それをはがきとして利用したのよ。

ジュディ：素晴らしい！　でも和紙を作るのは簡単ではないわ。もし私があなただったら，店ではがきを買うでしょうね。

京子　　：あのね…。あなたは伝統的な日本のものが大好きだから，私は和紙を使ってあなたのために特別なものを作りたかったの。どのようにすれば素敵な年賀状を作ることができるのかということを考えるのは楽しかったわ。

ジュディ：あなたの年賀状は素晴らしかったわ！　その年賀状は私に日本文化の興味深い部分を知る機会を与えてくれた。和紙はきれいであるだけでなく，あなたたちの文化の中で重要であることも知ったわ。

京子　　：あなたが和紙に関する新しいことを教えてくれたから，あなたとそれについて楽しく話せたわ。もしよければ，博物館へ行きましょう。次の日曜日は暇？

ジュディ：ええ，もちろん！

5．PICK UP (P. 60～72)

問答・応答

〈解答〉

1 (1) オ　(2) イ　(3) ク　(4) カ　(5) エ　(6) ア　(7) ウ　(8) キ

2 (1) ウ　(2) エ　(3) イ　(4) ウ

3 (1) ア　(2) イ　(3) エ

4 (1) エ　(2) エ　(3) ウ　(4) ア

5 (1) ウ　(2) ア　(3) エ　(4) ウ　(5) ウ　(6) ア

1 (1) Do you ～?で始まる疑問文には，Yes, I do./No, I don't.のいずれかで答える。(2) Whose は「誰の」と所有者を尋ねる疑問詞。It's Jasmine's.＝「それはジャスミンのものです」。(3) Are you（単数）～?で始まる疑問文には，Yes, I am./No, I'm not.のいずれかで答える。(4)「ご用でしょうか？（いらっしゃいませ）」―「はい。私は時計を探しています」。(5) Would you please ～?＝「～していただけませんか？」。Sure. No problem.＝「はい。いいですよ」。(6) What time は時間を尋ねる疑問詞。(7) 現在完了〈have＋過去分詞〉の疑問文には，have を用いて答える。(8) Shall we ～?＝「(一緒に) ～しましょうか？」。Yes, let's.＝「はい，そうしましょう」。

2 (1)「あなたは今までにヨーロッパでいくつの国を訪れたことがありますか？」―「3 つです。私はフランスと他 2 つを訪問したことがあります」。(2)「これはあなたのコンピューターですか，ミカ？」―「いいえ，私のは壊れています」。(3)「誕生日おめでとう，タケシ。これはあなたのためのものです」―「ありがとう。それを開けてもいいですか？」。May I ～?＝「～してもいいですか？」。(4)「昼食に出かけるのはどうですか？」―「ごめんなさい。私は友人に会うところです」。現在進行形で近い未来を表すことがある。

3 (1)「今夜夕食に出ましょうか？」→「はい，そうしましょう」。Shall we ～?の誘いかけに対しては，Yes, let's./No, let's not.などと答える。(2)「あなたは今までに彼に会ったことがありますか？」→「はい，あります」。現在完了の疑問文〈Have you ～?〉に対しては，Yes, I/we have.または，No, I/we haven't.で答える。(3)「あなたは誰がその試合に勝つと思いますか？」→「彼が勝つでしょう」。

4 (1)「今日，あなたは朝食に何を食べましたか？」という質問に対する返答。食事の内容を答えているものを選ぶ。(2)「私を手伝ってくれませんか？」という依頼に対する返答を選ぶ。Of course.＝「もちろんです」。(3)「この近くの駅はどこですか？」という質問に対する返答。B の「すみません」，「私はここの観光客なのです」ということばから，B は駅の場所を知らないと考えられる。(4)「二度と遅刻しないでください」ということばに対する返答。I won't be late.＝「私は遅刻しないつもりです」。

5 (1) B が手紙を出そうとしていて，A に料金をたずねていることから，A は郵便局の局員であると考えられる。ウの「何かお手伝いしましょうか？」が適切。(2) A が「買うべきものが見つかりませんでした」と答えていることから，アの「あなたは何か買いましたか？」が適切。(3) B が「あなたは何回その映画を見ましたか？」とたずねていることから，エの「3 回」が適切。(4) A が「それは 10,000 円でした」と答えていることから，ウの「それはいくらでしたか？」が適切。(5) A が「私はパスタを食べます」と答えていることから，ウを選んで「私はカレーライスを食べようと思います。あなたはどうですか？」とする。(6) A が B に土曜日の予定を聞き，そのあとで B を映画に誘っていることから考える。アの「私はまだ予定がありません」が適切。

絵や表を見て答える問題

〈解答〉

6 (1) エ　(2) エ

7 (1) ウ　(2) エ　(3) イ　(4) ア

8 ウ

9 (1) ウ　(2) ウ　(3) イ

10 (1) ① library　② museum　③ front　(2) ア. right　イ. left

11 (1) Shikoku　(2) will　(3) sunny（または，clear）　(4) in　(5) morning

12 (1) ア　(2) イ

13 (1) ウ　(2) イ　(3) ウ　(4) エ　(5) イ

6 (1) この店が閉まっているのは，週の何曜日か？→広告に「水曜日」が休業日と書かれている。(2) 客は無料で何をもらえるか？→広告に「無料のコーヒーがついたバナナケーキ」と書かれている。

【全訳】

ジンのケーキ店 開店時間：午前８時 30 分～午後７時 休業日：水曜日と正月休み 私たちの新しいチーズケーキをお試しください！ (50 セントだけの追加です) 無料のコーヒーがついたバナナケーキ 月曜日と金曜日のみ

7 ５文目の「ビーフステーキも最も人気のある料理の１つだが，カレーライスほど人気がない」から，カレーライスが(1)でビーフステーキは(2)である。６文目の「スパゲティの割合はビーフステーキの半分である」から，スパゲティは(4)。残ったピザが(3)である。

【全訳】 私たちは ABC レストランで，お気に入りの料理について 100 人にたずねました。このグラフはその割合を示しています。最も人気のある料理はチキンバーガーです。私たちはたくさんの若者がそれを好んでいると分かりました。ビーフステーキも最も人気のある料理のうちの１つですが，それはカレーライスほどは人気がありません。スパゲティの割合はビーフステーキの半分です。ピザは特に若い男性に人気があります。その他は例えば，チーズバーガー，ビーフシチューやサンドイッチです。

8 会話をしている時刻は８時で，日曜日には８時５分発のバスが運休なので，一番早いのは８時 30 分発のバスである。

【全訳】

ミカ：すみません。

ケン：はい。

ミカ：もうすでに８時ですが，バスがまだ来ません。なぜだかわかりますか？

ケン：あなたはどのバスを待っているのですか？

ミカ：このバスです。

ケン：ああ，今日は日曜日なので，そのバスは来ません。

ミカ：それでは，私はどのバスに乗ることができますか？

ケン：ええと，一番早いバスはこれですね。

ミカ：わかりました。それに乗ります。ありがとうございます。

9 (1) 映画は 10 時から 12 時 30 分までである。(2) ニュースが始まる時間は６時と 12 時 30 分。(3) ８時から始まる番組の説明に「パリの街で見られる衣服」と書かれている。

10 (1) ① ケンの説明より，地図上の星印からまっすぐ行って，３つ目の角に見えるのは図書館。② 地図より，病院は郵便局と博物館の間にある。③ 地図より，病院はレストランの前にある。in front of ～ =「～の前に」。(2) ア．病院へ行くには図書館のある角を「右」に曲がる必要がある。イ．図書館の前の道をまっすぐ歩いて行くと，病院は「左」にある。

11 (1) 絵より，午前中に雨が降るのは四国。(2) 明日のことなので未来形にする。will be ～ =「～になるでしょう」。(3) 絵より，関西では午後に「晴れる」。(4)・(5) 絵より，東北で雪が降るのは「午前」。in the morning =「午前に」。

【全訳】 では，お天気です。明日の午前中は四国と九州の一部で雨となりますが，午後は晴れるでしょう。関西地方は午前中少し曇りますが，のちに晴れるでしょう。関東地方は高気圧の中心に覆われ，一日中晴れるでしょう。東北では午前中少し雪が降るかもしれませんが，午後はよいお天気となるでしょう。北海道は午前は雪で午後にやみますが，今日はおそらく日差しはないでしょう。

12 (1) 数学が一番好きな生徒はどれぐらいいるか？→グラフを見ると，数学が一番好きな生徒は「15 %」をしめている。(2) 一番人気がある科目は何か？→グラフを見ると，「日本語（国語）」が最も多くの割合をしめている。

13 (1) 3月のカレンダーで，最も多く売り切れになっている曜日は金曜日。(2)「両親は週末しか空いていない」，「トムは日曜日の晩に空手のレッスンがある」という条件から考える。オペラは午後7時に開演するので，トムの家族が見に行けるのは土曜日の3月11日か3月25日。(3) C席の値段は1人あたり45ドル。学生のトムは10ドル引になるので，3人で125ドルになる。(4) D席に学生割引はない。また，団体割引があるのは5人以上の場合である。よって，学生を含む4人でD席のチケットを購入した場合，割引はない。(5) D席は2枚で60ドル。トムとナンシーがそれぞれB席のチケットを購入すれば，学生割引を受けて2名分で90ドルになるので，合計金額が150ドルになる。

【全訳】

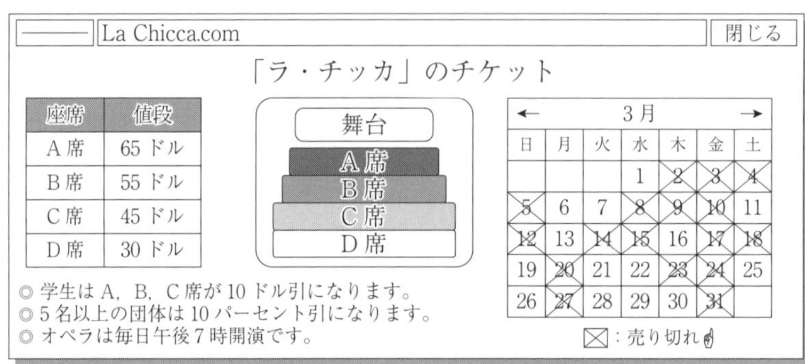

単　語

〈解答〉

14 (1) (f)ace　(2) (j)ob　(3) (v)egetable　(4) (m)eat　(5) (b)ody

15 (1) ウ　(2) ア

16 (1) zoo　(2) colors

17 (1) (p)assport　(2) (r)emember　(3) (n)inth　(4) (g)raduate　(5) (w)oke

18 (1) (s)eason　(2) (M)ay　(3) (h)ome（または，(h)ere）　(4) (W)ednesday

19 (1) February　(2) Saturday　(3) racket　(4) bat（または，bird）　(5) airport

20 (1) kitchen　(2) November　(3) lake　(4) umbrella　(5) summer　(6) hand　(7) uncle

21 (1) September　(2) doctor　(3) library　(4) dictionary

22 （ア，イの順に）(1) threw，through　(2) hear，here　(3) meet，meat　(4) clothes，close　(5) rode，road

14 (1) 目，鼻，口→「顔」。(2) 音楽家，医者，技術者→「職業」。(3) トマト，ニンジン，ジャガイモ→「野菜」。(4) 牛肉，鶏肉，豚肉→「肉」。(5) 手，脚，頭→「身体」。

15 (1) 字を書いたり絵を描いたりするための長いもの→「ペン」。(2) 多くの生徒が学校へ行くために乗り，歩く時間がない時に多くの人が使うもの→「自転車」。

16 (1) 私たちは多くの種類の動物を見るために「動物園」へ行きます。(2) 青，赤そして緑は「色」を表す語です。

17 (1)「パスポートを持っていなければ海外旅行はできません」。passport ＝「パスポート」。(2)「私の車の鍵がどこにあるか知っていますか？　それらをどこに置いたのか思い出せません」。remember ＝「思い出す」。(3)「9月は9番目の月です」。ninth ＝「9番目の」。(4)「大学を卒業したあと，私は外国企業で働きたいと思っています」。graduate from ～＝「～を卒業する」。(5)「私は今朝遅くに目が覚めて，バスに乗り遅れました」。wake up ＝「目が覚める」。wake の過去形は woke。

18 (1)「秋は1年の中で私の大好きな『季節』です」。(2)「『5月』は1年の中で5番目の月です」。(3)「私たちの先生は，もし私たちが具合が悪いなら『家』にいるように言った」。(4)「火曜日の後に『水曜日』が来ます」。

19 (1)「一年の2番目の月」は「2月」。(2)「金曜日のあとに来る日」は「土曜日」。(3)「私たちがテニスをするときに使うもの」は「ラケット」。(4)「空を飛ぶことができる動物」は「コウモリ」や「鳥」。(5)「人々が海外に行くために訪れる場所」は「空港」。

20 (1) 料理をしたり，皿を洗ったりするために使われる部屋→「台所」。(2) 10月と12月の間にある1年の11番目の月→「11月」。(3) 陸に囲まれた水の地域で，池よりも大きい→「湖」。(4) 雨や暑い日差しからあなた自身を守るために使うもの→「傘」。(5) 春と秋の間の1年で最も暖かい季節→「夏」。(6) 腕のはしにある身体の部分→「手」。(7) あなたの母親か父親の兄弟→「おじ」。

21 (1)「1年の9番目の月」→「9月」。(2)「病気のとき見てもらう必要がある人」→「医者」。(3)「本を借りたいときに行く場所」→「図書館」。(4)「ある言葉の意味が知りたい場合使うことができる本」→「辞書」。

22 (1) ア．彼はとても怒って，壁に彼のペンを「投げた」。イ．彼は部屋「を通り抜けて」台所へ行った。go through 〜 to …=「〜を通り抜けて…へ行く」。(2) ア．私はあなたの言ったことが「聞こえ」なかった。イ．彼は2日前に「ここに」来た。(3) ア．私たちは次の金曜日に駅の前で「会う」つもりだ。イ．私は昨夜，夕食に「肉」を食べた。(4) ア．私は毎日私の「服」を洗う。イ．出かけるときに，ドアを「閉めて」もらえませんか。(5) ア．高校生のとき，私は学校へバスに「乗っていった」。イ．「道路」にたくさんの車がある。

相関単語表

〈解答〉

23 (1) third (2) running (3) children (4) broken (5) best
24 (1) night (2) school (3) theirs (4) down (5) put
25 (1) thrown (2) left (3) knives (4) west (5) daughter
26 (1) cried (2) November (3) done (4) mine (5) best
27 (1) light (2) stories (3) drawn (4) themselves (5) peace
28 (1) its (2) won't (3) July (4) worst (5) different

23 (1) 序数詞を答える。「3番目の」= third。(2) 現在分詞形にする。run の現在分詞形は running。(3) 複数形にする。child の複数形は children。(4) 過去分詞形にする。break の過去分詞形は broken。(5) 最上級にする。good の最上級は best。

24 (1)「太陽」に対して「日中，昼間」。「月」に対して「夜」。(2)「医者」に対して「病院」。「教師」に対して「学校」。(3)「〜のもの」を表す所有代名詞にする。(4)「中へ」に対して「外へ」。「上へ」に対して「下へ」。(5) 過去形にする。put の過去形は put。

25 (1) 過去分詞にする。(2) 過去形にする。(3) 複数形にする。knife，life，wolf など，[f]の発音で終わる語を複数形にするときには，語尾の f，fe をとり，ves をつける。(4) 対義語を答える。east（東）の対義語は west（西）。(5) 対義語を答える。son（息子）の対義語は daughter（娘）。

26 (1) 過去形にする。〈子音字＋ y〉で終わる語の過去形は，y を i に変えて ed をつける。(2)「5」に対して「5月」。「11」に対して「11月」。(3) 過去分詞にする。(4) 所有代名詞にする。(5) 最上級にする。

27 (1)「短い」に対して「長い」。「重い」に対して「軽い」。(2) 複数形にする。story は語尾の y を i に変えて es をつけて複数形にする。(3) 過去分詞にする。draw - drew - drawn と活用する。(4)「私の」に対して「私自身」。「彼らの」の対して「彼ら自身」。(5) 発音が同じでつづりが異なるもの。piece の発音は[piːs]である。

28 (1) 所有格にする。(2) 短縮形にする。(3)「1番目」に対して「1月」。「7番目」に対して「7月」。(4) 最上級にする。bad は bad - worse - worst と変化する。(5)「暑い」に対して「寒い」。「同じ」に対して「異なった」。